Global Food Governance

Studies in Global Economic Law
Studien zum globalen Wirtschaftsrecht
Études en droit économique mondial

edited by Thomas Cottier

Volume 15

PETER LANG
Bern · Berlin · Bruxelles · Frankfurt am Main · New York · Oxford · Wien

Mariela Maidana-Eletti

Global Food Governance

Implications of Food Safety and Quality Standards in International Trade Law

PETER LANG
Bern · Berlin · Bruxelles · Frankfurt am Main · New York · Oxford · Wien

Bibliographic information published by die Deutsche Nationalbibliothek
Die Deutsche Nationalbibliothek lists this publication in the Deutsche Nationalbibliografie; detailed bibliographic data is available on the Internet at ‹http://dnb.d-nb.de›.

British Library Cataloguing-in-Publication Data: A catalogue record for this book is available from The British Library, Great Britain

Library of Congress Control Number: 2015959781

Luzerner Dissertation 2014.

ISSN 1423-9531 pb.
ISBN 978-3-0343-2009-2 pb.

ISSN 2235-7386 eBook
ISBN 978-3-0351-0917-7 eBook

This publication has been peer reviewed.

Hochfeldstrasse 32, CH-3012 Bern, Switzerland
info@peterlang.com, www.peterlang.com

In Memoriam of
Adriana Eletti de Maidana
(1947–2000)

Acknowledgement

This book is the product of my PhD research, carried out while working part-time as a research and teaching assistant at the Department of Public and Rural Law at the University of Lucerne, School of Law, under the aegis of Prof. Roland Norer – who kindly agreed to act as my PhD supervisor.

During this academic journey, which started in late 2009 and culminated with the successful defense of the thesis in December 2014, I had the opportunity to meet many accomplished and inspiring individuals. These encounters shaped and influenced not only my legal research, but also my professional and personal outlook about the meaning of being a lawyer and becoming part of the legal academic community.

In particular, this work would have not been possible without the constant professional support offered by Prof. Roland Norer, Prof. Bernhard Rütsche and Prof. Alexander Morawa at the University of Lucerne. I am especially thankful to Prof. Alberto Alemanno at HEC Paris and New York University, for acting as my external examiner and to Prof. Bernd van der Meulen at Wageningen University, for fruitful discussions at the early stages of this research. I acknowledge the generous financial support from the Swiss National Science Foundation (SNSF) under the Fellowship for Prospective Researchers, as well as funding provided by the Research Commission at the University of Lucerne.

Some chapters of this work were researched and drafted at the Food Law Department of the Swiss Federal Ministry of Public Health in Berne, during the 2010 revision period of most acts and ordinances on Swiss food law. I had the opportunity to experience first-hand the legal implications of the autonomous implementation of EU law and the introduction of the Cassis-de-Dijon principle in the Swiss food legal system. I am grateful to Peter Perinat for his trust and support. I am particularly grateful to Adrian Kunz, for constantly sharing his unmatched knowledge of Swiss food law with me.

This thesis was revised after the viva voce in accordance with the PhD Committee's suggestions. I was fortunate enough to conduct the

PhD review at the World Trade Institute, University of Berne, where I could benefit not only from the thriving academic environment but also from one of the largest specialized libraries in international economic law. The publication of this thesis would have not been possible without the support of Prof. Thomas Cottier, who kindly agreed to review and accept this manuscript in the Global Economic Law Series with Peter Lang Publishers.

I am also in debt to Dr. Patrick Fassbind, Marco Ferrari, Marc Suter, Gerhard Hauser-Schönbächler and Antoinette Blaser, for showing me the ropes in Swiss legal practice. The daily challenges, as well as the immense satisfaction, of practicing law have helped me putting into perspective the theoretical implications of the research we carry out in the "ivory tower".

Lastly, this work would have not seen the light without the unconditional moral and emotional support of my family. I am grateful to Martin Amstalden, Adalberto Maidana-Diaz, Milagros Alonso-Botran, Daniela Maidana-Eletti, Fernando Maidana-Eletti, Adrian Maidana-Eletti, Monica Amstalden, Fritz Meroz and Remo Amstalden for walking by my side during this journey and so many others. I am blessed to be part of your life.

I dedicate this book to my late mother Adriana, my guiding star.

Mariela Maidana-Eletti
Georgetown, Washington DC in August 2015

Table of Contents

List of Abbreviations

AB	(WTO) Appellate Body
AG	Aktiengesellschaft
AIDCO	Agreement on International Dolphin Conservation Program
Appl. Econ. P. Pol.	Oxford Journal of Applied Economic Perspectives and Policy
Art./s	Article/s
ASEAN	Association of Southeast Asian Nations
BGBl.	(German) Bundesgesetzblatt
BMELV	Bundesministerium für Ernährung und Landwirtschaft
BRC	British Retail Consortium
BSE	Bovine Spongiform Encephalopathy
BVerwG	Bundesverwaltungsgericht/German Federal Administrative Court
C	Case
CAC	Codex Alimentarius Commission
CDIP	WIPO Committee on Development and Intellectual Property
Cf.	Confer
Co.	Company
COM	Communication
Conf.	Conference
COOL	Country of Origin Labelling
Cth	Commonwealth of Australia
Dir.	(EU) Directive
Doc.	Document
DS	WTO Dispute Settlement
e.g.	exemplia gratia/for example
EC	European Communities
EEC	European Economic Community
ECJ	European Court of Justice

ECR	European Communities Report
ed/eds	Editor/s
EFSA	European Food Safety Authority
EFTA	European Free Trade Association
EG	Europäische Gemeinschaft
et al.	et alibi/and others
et seq.	et sequens/and that which follows
EU	European Union
FAO	Food and Agriculture Organisation
FCTC	WHO Framework Convention on Tobacco Control
FDFA	Swiss Federal Department of Foreign Affairs
fr.	French
FTA	Free Trade Agreement
GAP	Good Agricultural Practices
GATT	General Agreement on Tariffs and Trade
ger.	German
GFSI	Global Food Safety Initiative
GlobalGAP	Global Partnership for Good Agricultural Practices
IFG	(German) Informationsfreiheitsgesetz
IFS	International Food Standard
Inc.	Incorporation
IPPC	International Plant Protection Convention
ISA	International Federation of the National Standardizing Associations
ISO	International Organization for Standardization
Iss.	Issue
LBFG	(German) Lebensmittel-, Bedarfsgegenstände- und Futtermittelgesetzbuch
Ltd.	Limited
MERCOSUR	Mercado Común del Sur
MIT	Massachusetts Institute of Technology
NAFTA	North American Free Trade Agreement
Nr.	Number
NWF	Nordrhein-Westfalen
OECD	Organization for Economic Cooperation and Development

OIE	Office International des Epizooties
OJ	EU Official Journal
OVG	Oberverwaltungsgericht
p./pp.	page/s
para./s	paragraph/s
R	(WTO) Report
RASFF	Rapid Alert System for Foodstuffs
Rev.	Revised
S.	Seite
s./ss.	Section/s
SPS Agreement	WTO Agreement on Sanitary and Phytosanitary Measures
SQF	Safe Quality Food
SR	Systematische Sammlung des Bundesrechts
TBT Agreement	WTO Agreement on Technical Barriers to Trade
THG	(Swiss) Bundesgesetz über die technischen Handelshemmnisse
TRIPS Agreement	WTO Agreement on Trade-Related Aspects of Intellectual Property Rights
TS	Technical Specification
UK	United Kingdom of Great Britain and Northern Ireland
UN	United Nations
UNDP	United Nations Development Program
UNIDO	United Nations Industrial Development Organization
UNSCC	United Nations Standards Coordinating Committee
UNTS	United Nation Treaty Series
US	United States of America
v.	versus
VG	(German) Verwaltungsgericht
VIPaV	(Swiss) Verordnung über das Inverkehrbringen von nach ausländischen technischen Vorschriften hergestellten Produkten und über deren Überwachung auf dem Markt
VO	(EU) Verordnung

Vol.	Volume
WHO	World Health Organization
WIPO	World Intellectual Property Organization
WTO	World Trade Organisation
ZAR	Zeitschrift für Arbeitsrecht

Introduction

1. Global Food Markets and Standards

As globalised markets, changing consumer preferences and the steady development of new technologies influence food trade flows, safety and quality concerns have triggered the development of new forms of food governance. Likewise, the expanding global food market continues to increase the economic value of world food exports and imports, which already reached US 1,375 billion in 2012 alone.[1] While the European Union tops the list of leading food markets with US 522 billion dollars in exports, the United States follows in the second place with US 138 billion dollars.[2] Switzerland remains an important market player with an increase of over 300% in food exports since 2000, accounting for a total value of US 8,414 million dollars in 2012.[3] The tendency in global food trade is set to increase, albeit slightly more slowly, in the coming years.[4]

As a result of these market fluctuations, recent decades have seen significant changes in the legal architecture governing trade in food. Since its creation in 1995, the World Trade Organization (WTO) has succeeded in providing a multilateral framework for the development of new regulatory practices through its multiple agreements between WTO Members. Similarly, the continuing importance of regional and bilateral trade agreements has enhanced these accomplishments, proving a comprehensive and dynamic set of international rules and standards for trade in foodstuffs. However, the changing trends in the production and distribution

1 World Trade Organization, International Trade Statistics 2013, <www.wto.org/statistics> (last visited: 30 June 2015), p. 70 [WTO, International Trade Statistics 2013].

2 WTO International Trade Statistics 2013, p. 72.

3 WTO International Trade Statistics 2013, p. 73.

4 OECD/FAO, OECD/FAO Agricultural Outlook 2013–2022, <http://www.agri-outlook.org> (last visited: 30 June 2015).

of food products and recent worldwide outbreaks of food-borne diseases have questioned the effectiveness of the current regulatory status quo.[5]

While international trade in food increases, national governments remain at times unable to regulate food products and food industries effectively. Transnational competition, increasing corporate power and the consolidation of global food industries require collective policy action that can no longer be attained on a domestic level alone.[6] Equally, the legal implications of food safety and quality standards in designing effective trade policies cannot be overseen.

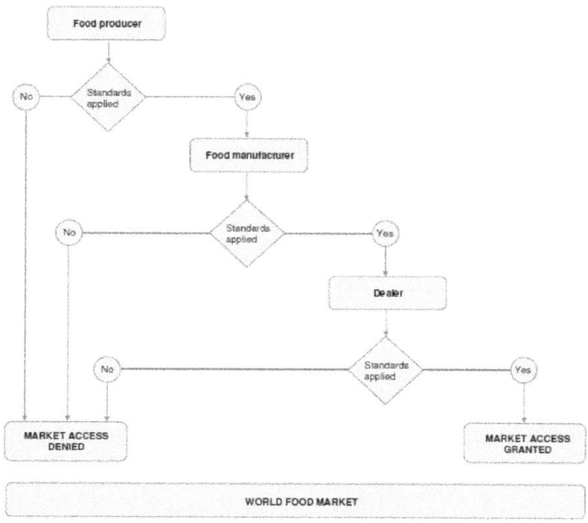

Figure 1: The Role of Food Standards in International Trade.

Source: Author

5 World Health Organization, Global Strategy for Food Safety, Food Safety Programs, Geneva, WHO 2002 [WHO, Global Strategy for Food Safety]. On the globalisation of food markets see generally *inter alia*: David Vogel, Trading Up: Consumer and Environmental Regulation in a Global Economy, Harvard University Press 1995; David Held, Global Transformation, Stanford University Press 1999.

6 See *e.g.*: Genaro Garcia/Reba Carruth, 'Multilateral Governance of Food Safety in Global Food Industries and Food Systems: The Role of FAO, WHO and Codex Alimentarius in Regulatory Harmonization' in: Reba Carruth (ed), Global Governance of Food and Agriculture Industries: Transatlantic Regulatory Harmonization and Multilateral Policy Cooperation for Food Safety, Edward Elgar 2006, pp. 392–430.

As the figure above shows, food standards display potential trade-enhancing and trade-distorting effects, and thus are being closely scrutinised on international, regional and domestic levels in terms of their scientific justification and economic efficiency.[7] While attempting to reduce the trade-distorting effects of differing food standards, three main regulatory approaches have been created to overcome trade obstacles: coordination, harmonisation and equivalence or mutual recognition.[8] It is against this backdrop that this thesis aims at addressing the advantages gained and the challenges posed by the emergence of new forms of global food governance.

2. Hypothesis and Methodology

New governance mechanisms are rapidly evolving to ensure that global food demands are met. The result is an increasingly complex network of international food standards influencing trade law. This thesis is therefore based on a review of legal, political and economic literature, from which it became evident that extensive research has been carried out to address the social and economic implications of food standards in international trade. However, research on the legal aspects of the current global architecture for food governance, particularly with regard to the role of international standards, is still very much in its infancy. In the absence of a comprehensive legal analysis of private and public food safety and quality standards, this work aims at reconceptualising some of the implications of food standards in international trade law.

Therefore, the underlying research question is: what are the legal implications of food safety and quality standards for international trade law? The hypothesis is that food standards have acquired a prominent place in the legal architecture of rules governing trade in food, and have thus triggered the creation of new forms of governance designed to meet

7 Gary Smith, 'Interaction of Public and Private Standards in the Food Chain' OECD Food, Agriculture and Fisheries Working Papers Nr. 15, OECD Publishing 2009, AGR/CA/APM(2006)21/final [Smith].

8 Smith, para. 64.

the demands of food producers and global food markets. It addresses the legal implications of food safety and quality standards based on three regulatory approaches: harmonisation (WTO), cooperation (European Union [EU]) and mutual recognition or equivalence (Switzerland).

Methodologically, this work draws from findings in the legal field as well as from economic and social sciences. In essence, this thesis aims at covering the following aspects:

- Legal theory and social sciences in general

The first chapter addresses the evolution of good governance as a legal concept. It will predominantly make use of the general methodology developed in legal theory to identify the essential elements for the analysis and understanding of the subsequent sections.

- Legal doctrine

The thesis will be strongly influenced by a doctrinal approach. This includes the selection of materials, their analysis and inclusion in larger contexts of international economic law. It also includes the systematization and consolidation of the current legal framework for food standards.

- Case law analysis

The international legal framework for food law will be researched through case law analysis. Relevant WTO provisions as well as European and Swiss rules will be complemented by an analysis of the work carried out by the WTO dispute settlement system, the European Court of Justice (ECJ) and selected domestic courts.

- Comparative law

The thesis will be throughout conducted according to legal comparative practices. In doing so, the similarities and differences between the legal standing of food standards in the WTO, EU and in Switzerland will be continuously compared and analysed.

- Interdisciplinarity

The purpose of this thesis is directed towards an integrated examination of international food law and trade. The existing legal fragmentation at international and national levels will be levelled through an interdisciplinary but coherent methodology that includes the latest developments in food standards from the legal, but also political and economic sciences.

This current work differs from previous ones because it focuses on the existing jurisprudence addressing (food) standards, instead of creating new, untested policy considerations. By concluding that the normative nature of food standards does not constitute a determining factor in assessing the applicability of the relevant legal instruments, this work adds to the academic literature on international trade law in general and food standardisation in particular.

Chapter 1 will examine the basics underlying global food governance by defining the concept of good governance, global governance and food governance, examining those theoretical categories and developing a core definition based on those codings. Once the scope of the research has been identified, through a grounded-theory approach and with caveats aside, an examination of the most important principles underlying the economic theory of free trade (albeit non-exhaustive in character) will shed light onto the foundations of WTO law.

1. Global Food Governance

1.1 Exploring the Concept of Global Governance

The concept of governance was first identified in and limited to the field of economics, where it rapidly gained relevance.[9] In the past two decades, however, this term has passed its own conceptual boundaries[10] to become a widely-used term in describing the conduct of world affairs across different disciplines.[11] It has also been defined as a technocratic process that follows the efficiency dogma,[12] as the process of running a government and other public and private agencies with a social purpose,[13] as a term

9 See *inter alia*: OECD, Corporate Governance: Improving Competitiveness and Access to Capital in Global Markets, OECD, Paris 1998; DONALD CHEW, Studies in International Corporate Finance and Governance Systems – A Comparison of the US, Japan and Europe, Oxford University Press 1997; OLIVER WILLIAMSON, 'The Economics of Governance: Framework and Implications' (1984) 140 Zeitschrift für die gesamte Staatswissenschaft, pp. 195–223; MORTEN BOAS, 'Governance as Multilateral Bank policy: The Cases of the African Development Bank and the Asian Development Bank' (1998) 10 (2) European Journal of Development Research, pp. 117–134.

10 On the origins of the term 'Global Governance' see *generally*: JAMES ROSENAU, 'Governance, Order, and Change in World Politics' in: JAMES ROSENAU/ERNST-OTTO CZEMPOIEL (eds), Governance without Government: Order and Change in World Politics, Cambridge University Press 1992, pp. 1–29; JAN KOOIMAN, 'Findings, Recommendations and Speculations' in: JAN KOOIMAN (ed), Modern Governance: New Government-Society Interactions, Sage 1993, pp. 249–262.

11 MARTIN HEWSON/TIMOTHY SINCLAIR, 'The Emergence of Global Governance Theory' in: MARTIN HEWSON/TIMOTHY SINCLAIR (eds), Global Governance Theory, State University of New York Press 1999, pp. 3–22, p. 3.

12 ROBERT LATHAM, 'Politics in a Floating World' in: MARTIN HEWSON/TIMOTHY SINCLAIR (eds), Global Governance Theory, State University of New York Press 1999, pp. 23–54.

13 GORAN HYDEN, 'Governance and the Study of Politics' in: GORAN HYDEN/MICHAEL BRATTON (eds), Governance and Politics in Africa, Lynne Rienner 1992, pp. 1–26.

for contemporary global problem solving,[14] as a means of reference for the era after the breakdown of European Socialism in 1989[15] and as a formula that verbalizes '[the] overlapping of different disciplinary perspectives in a collaborative effort to make sense of the transformation associated with globalization'.[16]

The Commission on Global Governance defined the term as:

> [Global Governance] is the sum of the many ways individuals and institutions, private and public, manage their common affairs. It is the continuing process through which conflicting or diverse interests may be accommodated and co-operative action may be taken.[17]

For a regional perspective, the European Commission understood governance as:[18]

14 See *generally*: Mihaly Simai, The Future of Global Governance: Managing Risks and Change in the International System, US Institute of Peace 1994; Meghnad Desai/Paul Redfern (eds), Global Governance: Ethics and Economics of the World Order, Printer 1995; Richard Falk, On Humane Governance, Penn State Press 1995; Paul Diehl (ed), The Politics of Global Governance: International Organizations in an Independent World, Lynne Rienner 1997.

15 See *generally*: Christian Gerlach, 'Illusions of Global Governance: Transnational Agribusiness inside the UN System' in: Alexander Nützenadel/Frank Trentmann, Food and Globalization: Consumption, Markets and Politics in the Modern World, Berg Publishers 2008, pp. 193–211; Armin von Bogdandy/Philipp Dann/Matthias Goldmann, 'Developing the Publicness of Public International Law: Towards a Legal Framework for Global Governance Activities' in: Armin von Bogdandy/Rüdiger Wolfrum/Jochen von Bernstorff/Philipp Dann/Matthias Goldmann (eds), The Exercise of Public Authority by International Institutions, Springer 2006, pp. 3–32.

16 Peer Zumbansen, 'The Incurable Constitutional Itch: Transnational Private Regulatory Governance and the Woes of Legitimacy', King's Collge London Dickson Poon School of Law Legal Studies Research Paper Series, Nr. 2014–40, p. 21.

17 Commission on Global Governance, Our Global Neighborhood, Oxford University Press 1995, p. 2.

18 See *generally*: Les Metcalfe, 'Reforming the European Governance: Old Problems or New Principles?' (2001) 67 International Review of Administrative Sciences, pp. 415–443; Fritz Scharpf, 'European Governance: Common Concerns vs. the Challenge of Diversity' in: Markus Jachtenfuchs/Michelle Knodt (eds), Regieren in Internationalen Institutionen, Springer 2002, pp. 271–284; Christoph Möllers, 'European Governance: Meaning and Value of a Concept' (2006) 43 Common Market Law Review, pp. 313–336; Charles Sabel/

> the rules, processes and behaviour that affect the way in which powers are exercised [at European level], particularly as regards to openness, participation, accountability, effectiveness and coherence.[19]

European institutions have put this term into action by signing an Inter-Institutional Agreement on Better Law-Making,[20] whereby alternative regulation mechanisms, such as co-regulation and self-regulation, are preferred to legislation.[21]

However, governance does not only refer to different methods of regulation, but also to the shift in the allocation of authority from the top down,[22] where all the participating players in society pursue common goals through the exercise of control. In its most basic state, global governance determines and enforces a wide variety of governmental and non-governmental rules for the provision of public goods and services.[23] It is the latter definition of governance, one that encompasses governmental regulation as well as non-governmental rules, the one followed in the present study.

JONATHAN ZEITLIN, 'Learning from Difference: The New Architecture of Experimentalist Governance in the EU' (2008) 14 European Law Journal, pp. 271–327; CHIRSTIAN JOERGES, 'Integration Through De-legalisation?' (2008) 33 European Law Review, pp. 291–312.

19 EUROPEAN COMMISSION, European Governance: A White Paper, COM(201) 428 final, OJ C 287/1, 25 July 2001, pp. 7–8 [White Paper on European Governance].

20 EUROPEAN PARLIAMENT, COUNCIL AND COMMISSION, Inter-Institutional Agreement on Better Law-Making [2003] OJ C 321/01, 31 December 2003 [EU Agreement on Better Law-Making].

21 EU Agreement on Better Law-Making, para. 16. See *also*: LINDA SENDEN, 'Soft Law, Self-Regulation and Co-Regulation in European Law: Where do They Meet?' (2005) 9(1) Electronic Journal of Comparative Law, pp. 1–27; DAVID CHALMERS, 'Private Power and Public Authority in European Union Law' (2005–6) 8 Cambridge Yearbook of European Legal Studies, pp. 59–94.

22 See *generally*: ORAN YOUNG, International Governance: Protecting the Environment in a Stateless Society, Cornell University Press 1994; PHILIPP CERNY, 'Globalization and the Changing Logic of Collective Action' (1995) 49 (4) International Organizations, pp. 595–621.

23 ROBERT LAWRENCE, 'Comment on Gary C. Hufbauer' in: HORST SIEBERT (ed), Global Governance: An Architecture for the World Economy, Springer 2003, pp. 270–274, p. 271.

1.1.1 On Good Governance

Indeed, since the early 1980s, the concept of governance has permeated development discourse and research agendas.[24] The same dynamic applies to the concept of 'good governance', with subtantial variations in its definition, depending on the institutional body involved. While the World Bank refers to good governance as a politically effective exercise of power,[25] the definition drafted by the Organization for Economic Cooperation and Development (OECD) denotes a focus on a government's ability to design an economically effective framework for the distribution of resources.[26] In turn, the United Nations Development Programme (UNDP) conceptualised good governance as a comprehensive set of rules and procedures embedded in the rule of law.[27]

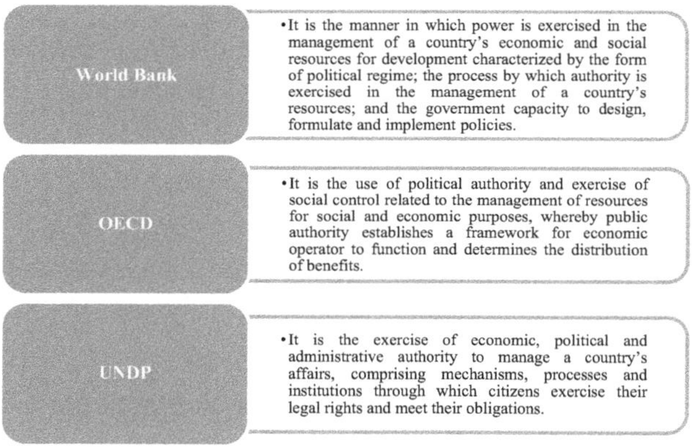

Figure 2: Definitions of Good Governance.

Source: Weiss, p. 392.

24 Thomas Weiss, 'Governance, Good Governance and Global Governance: Conceptual and Actual Changes', (2000) 21 (5) Third World Quarterly, pp. 795–814 [Weiss].

25 World Bank, Governance – The World Bank's Experience, The World Bank 1994, p. 14.

26 Organization for Economic Cooperation and Development (OECD), Participatory Development and Good Governance, Paris OECD 1994, p. 14.

27 United Nations Development Program (UNDP), 'Governance for Sustainable Development: Integrating Governance in the Post-2015 Development Framework, Discussion Paper' March 2014, p. 3.

In other words, global good governance refers to a complex set of rules, including regulations and standards, laid down by international institutions and private bodies that go beyond the realm of public policy in order to attain the ultimate common good. This definition is characterised by a horizontal approach to governance activities that renders the traditional vertical division between international, regional and national regulation and rules obsolete. In this sense, the concept of global good governance preferred in the current thesis does not follow the definition of governance as understood by the European Commission.[28] Thus, the present research will only make limited reference to the deficiencies arising out of the different governance mechanisms, and thus excludes any exhaustive analysis about legitimacy and transparency concerns[29] in the international standard-setting process.

1.1.2 On Food Governance

In line with the definition of global good governance identified above, the underlying premise of this research is a normative approach to global *food* governance, understood as a cooperative interplay of legal entities (public and private) to design and adopt harmonised rules that enhance international trade in food and so guarantee market access. Indeed, for foodstuffs to be placed in a global market, certain requirements must be fulfilled.

Food governance offers two main processes to guarantee market access: standard development and conformity assessment. Standard development provides food manufacturers with specific standards designed by a standard-setting body in accordance with a defined set of rules.[30] Conformity assessment procedures aim at ensuring the implementation of

28 White Paper on European Governance, pp. 7–8.

29 For an overview on the legitimacy concerns raised within the WTO see *inter alia*: Robert Howse/Kalypso Nicolaidis, 'Enhancing WTO Legitimacy: Constitutionalization or Global Subsidiarity?' (2003) 16 Governance, pp. 73–94; Amichai Cohen, 'Bureaucratic Internationalization: Domestic Governmental Agencies and the Legitimization of International Law' (2005) 30 Georgetown Journal of International Law, pp. 1079–1144.

30 Maki Hatanaka, 'Assessing Rule-Based Governance Mechanisms in an Era of Scientism' (2011) 25 (3) Journal of Rural Sciences, pp. 141–159.

standards by independent and objective bodies (i.e. third-party certifiers). These bodies generally use audits as a technical and objective conformity-assessment mechanism to ensure standards compliance.[31] The present study addresses the legal implications of the first element of food governance only,[32] that is, standard development. By doing so, it examines its three main pillars of standard development: standards, standard-setting bodies and, to a lesser extent, standard-setting processes.

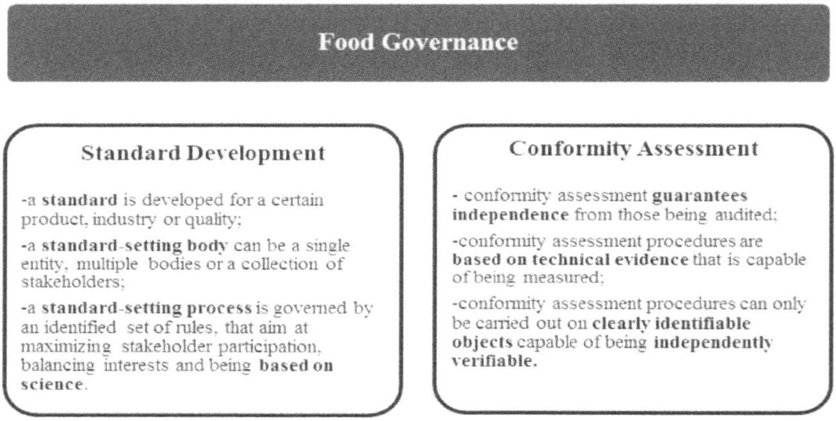

Figure 3: Elements of Food Governance.

Source: Author

Along this line, the tendency that has been identified here[33] defines governance mechanisms as being based on 'neo-corporatist regulatory

31 See *generally:* MICHAEL POWER, The Audit Society: Rituals of Verification, Oxford University Press 1997. See *also*: SASHA COURVILLE/CHRISTINE PARKER/HELEN WATCHIRS, 'Introduction: Auditing in Regulatory Perspective' (2003) 25 (3) Law & Policy, pp. 179–184.

32 For an analysis on conformity assessment procedures from a legal perspective see *generally*: ARTHUR APPLETON, 'Conformity Assessment Procedures' in: TRACEY EPPS/MICHAEL TREBILCOCK (eds), Research Handbook on the WTO and Technical Barriers to Trade, Edward Elgar 2013, pp. 81–119. For an economic perspective see *inter alia*: SHERRY SHEPHERSON, Standards, Conformity Assessment and Developing Countries, The World Bank 1997.

33 JAMES MCCARTHY/SCOOT PRUDHAM, 'Neoliberal Nature and the Nature of Neoliberalism' (2004) 35 (3) Geoforum 35, pp. 275–283, p. 276 [MCCARTHY/PRUDHAM].

frameworks involving non-binding standards and rules, public-private co-operation [and] self-regulation'.[34] In other words, a new legal architecture composed by elements of soft and hard law emerges to address the shortcomings of classic regulatory approaches, in times when the market drives regulatory change, and science is used as a basis for standard development, multiple global players share regulatory responsibility.[35] Hence, the fundamental role of food standards, understood in the wider sense as all rules affecting foodstuffs ('standards' in this literature) in the formation of new forms of governance is undeniable.

Indeed, the newest forms of governance, or so-called *experimentalist governance* by De Burca and others –[36] is described as:

> [A] set of practices involving open participation by a variety of entities (public and private), lack of formal hierarchy within governance arrangements, and extensive deliberation throughout the process of decision-making and implementation.[37]

Unlike older forms of governance, characterized by traditionally integrated international regimes[38] and global administrative law,[39] experimentalist governance does not aim at setting binding and definitive rules, but

34 McCarthy/Prudham, p. 276.

35 Allison Loconto/Lawrence Busch, 'Standards, Techno-Economic Networks, and Playing Fields: Performing the Global Market Economy' (2010) 17 Review of International Political Economy, pp. 507–536.

36 Grainne De Burca/Robert Keohane/Charles Sabel, 'New Modes of Pluralist Global Governance' New York University, School of Law, Public Law and Legal Theory Research Paper Working Series, Working Paper Nr. 13–08, March 2013, p. 16 [De Burca *et al.*].

37 De Burca *et al.*, p. 16.

38 These regimes are characterized in terms of a principle-agent model, whereby '*the leading nation-states [...] can be considered as principals who create international regimes to act as their agents in addressing and solving what are considered to be well defined governance problems arising from interdependence*'; De Burca *et al.*, p. 7.

39 De Burca *et al.* understood global administrative law as '*a bundle of principles, rules and practices derived from or analogous to principles of domestic administrative law, including due process, proportionality, judicial review and transparency*', p. 15.

instead, provisional goals and procedures for periodical peer-review to attain an ultimate objective.[40]

Based on the different legal and political theories of governance, it is feasible to define the concept of global food governance (also 'new forms of food governance' in this literature) as a *complex set of rules*, laid down by state and non-state actors that go beyond the realm of public policy in order to attain an ultimate common good, that is, the free flow of international trade in foodstuffs.

Because food standards act as an essential levelling mechanism for global food markets, it is necessary to review the theories underlying international trade, to later assess whether food governance is the result of a market failure or of granted market access.

1.2 Economic Theories of International Trade: A Question of Market Failure or Market Access?

1.2.1 Market Access

It has long been claimed that globalised free trade is only possible by implementing the theory of comparative advantage.[41] This argument has been put forward for centuries now, first by *Ricardo*[42] and then his followers. According to this theory, the main aim of regulators must be the reduction of obstacles for cross-border transactions, thus facilitating specialisation based on the division of labour. In turn, competition would increase among market actors and thus reduce prices.

It follows then, that market access will constitute the ultimate goal pursued by the theory of competitive advantage. Described as the totality of government-imposed conditions under which a product may enter

40 De Burca *et al.*, p. 20.

41 Paul Krugman, 'Is Free Trade Passe?' (1987) 1 (2) Journal of Economic Perspectives, pp. 131–144, p. 132.

42 See *generally*: David Ricardo, The Principles of Political Economy and Taxation, 1819, reprinted by Dent & Sons Ltd./Charles E. Tuttle Co. 1973.

a country,[43] market access is an ambiguous term that is referred to as a principle, a general right or a specific concession.[44] Hence, state obligations will vary depending on the legal status attributed to the concept of market access. While being applied as a principle will not necessarily impose positive obligations upon states, market access as a specific concession will inevitably lead to the amendment of domestic regulation in order to comply with international obligations.[45] Therefore, divergent standards with varied levels of implementation have the inherent potential of hindering market access, and thus continue to pose challenges in the formation of new forms of experimentalist governance. Likewise, harmonised food standards display trade-enhancing effects that render them highly effective in globalized food markets.

1.2.2 Market Failure

Unlike the economic theory of laissez-faire, whereby government regulation would pursue the ultimate aim of achieving a Pareto optimum, the legal theory of international trade focuses on providing a set of rules that legitimise government intervention addressing market failures.[46] Due to the inherent imperfection of markets, the achievement of a welfare society through free trade may initially appear an oxymoron. Regulators and rule-making bodies need to intervene as guarantors of social welfare in cases where markets fail to adjust the flow of free trade. It is to solve this market failure of information asymmetry that trade rules

43 World Trade Organization, Training Package, Goods: Market Access, WTO 1998.

44 John Mo, 'The Mystery of Market Access' in: Asif Qureshi/Xuan Gao, International Economic Law – Critical Concepts in Law, Vol. III, World Trade Law, Routledge 2010, pp. 50–76, p. 68 [Mo].

45 Mo argues that the mixed meanings used for market access are counter-productive in that it makes it difficult to assess what States actually mean while negotiating international treaties, pp. 70–71.

46 Paul Krugman, 'The Narrow and Broad Arguments for Free Trade' (1993) 83 (2) The American Economic Review, pp. 362–366, p. 366 [Krugman, Arguments for Free Trade]; see *also*: Paul Krugman, Strategic Trade Policy and the New International Economics, MIT Press 1986.

were created.[47] Certainly, the hypothesis that markets fail when information about the quality (and hence, safety) of a product is not readily available to consumers was already put forward many decades ago.[48]

From mercantilism[49] to more liberal trade policies,[50] modern trade law aims at going beyond the implementation of economic theories. Prior to the establishment of the WTO, however,[51] trade law was largely consigned to a group of policy measures aimed at implementing, but not completing, economic theories. Yet a globalised, open trading system has made the synergy between law and economics inevitable. An effective legal framework had to be put in place to guarantee certainty and coherence among the already functioning bodies embedded in public international law.[52] Indeed, it was during the Uruguay Round that international trade policies shifted from shallow to deep integration.[53] Until 1995, shallow integration was pursued to reduce or eliminate tariffs barriers.[54] After the Uruguay Round, trade policies shifted towards

47 KRUGMAN, Arguments for Free Trade, p. 363.

48 GEORGE ACKERLOF, 'The Market for "Lemons": Quality Uncertainties and the Market Mechanism' (1970) 84 Quarterly Journal of Economics, pp. 488–500.

49 This school argued that a favourable balance of trade was only guaranteed by close state intervention and reciprocal trade policies. An example of French policy recommendations can be seen in: JEAN-BAPTISTE COLBERT, Memorandum on Trade, 1664, reprinted by KRAUS, NENDELN (Lichtenstein) 1979; for an English example see: WILLIAM CUNNINGHAM, The Growth of English Industry and Commerce during the Early and Middle Ages, Cambridge, At the University Press 1882; for an overview on the current debate on protectionism see *generally*: IAN FLETCHER, Free Trade Doesn't Work: What Should Replace It and Why, US Business and Industry Council 2011.

50 See *e.g.* the theory of absolute advantage developed by ADAM SMITH, An Inquiry into the Nature and Causes of the Wealth of Nations, 1776, reprinted by Random House, Inc./Modern Library Ed. 1994.

51 Marrakesh Agreement Establishing the World Trade Organization, 1 January 1995, 1867 UNTS 154 [WTO Agreements].

52 For an overview of classical theory of trade law see *generally*: DOUGLAS IRWIN, Against the Tide: An Intellectual History of Free Trade, Princeton University Press 1996; evaluating the different theories of international trade see: PERLMAN MARK, The Pillars of Economic Understanding: Ideas and Traditions, The University of Michigan Press 1998.

53 SIMON LESTER/BRYAN MERCURIO/ARWEL DAVIES/KARA LEITNER, World Trade Law, Hart Publishing 2008, p. 59 [LESTER *et al.*].

54 LESTER *et al.*, p. 59.

deep integration, whereby the goal was rule harmonisation.[55] One of the most effective ways of harmonising and coordinating divergent rules is through standardisation. Food standards in international trade provide an accurate example of the benefits and challenges posed by such an endevour. In fact, the WTO Dispute Settlement system proved to be the most effective means available to review food trade measures that stem from divergent food safety and quality standards.[56] Without intending to be exhaustive and for the reader's convenience, the next section will highlight the basic legal principles underlying the current multilateral trading system.

1.3 A Summary of the Legal Foundations of the Multilateral Trading System

The foundation of the multilateral trading system is enshrined in six basic principles that are embedded in every WTO agreement. Non-discrimination, open markets, predictability and transparency, competitiveness, protection of the environment and support for the less developed countries are the leading objectives advocated and followed by the WTO regime.[57] Particularly relevant in assessing the impact of food standards in international trade are the non-discriminatory provisions found in the General Agreement on Tariffs and Trade (GATT)[58] – acting as the WTO

55 LESTER *et al.*, p. 59.

56 JILL HOBBS, 'Public and Private Standards for Food Safety and Quality: International Trade Implications' (2010) 11 (1) The Estey Centre Journal of International Law and Trade Policy, pp. 136–152.

57 WORLD TRADE ORGANIZATION, Understanding the WTO, Geneva 2011, pp. 10–13. See *generally*: MICHAEL TREBILCOCK/ROBERT HOWSE/ANTONIA ELIASON, The Regulation of International Trade, 4th ed., Routledge 2013 [TREBILCOCK *et al.*]; ANDREW MITCHELL, Legal Principles in WTO Disputes, Cambridge University Press 2008; ANDREW LANG, World Trade Law after Neoliberalism: Reimagining the Global Economic Order, Oxford University Press 2011.

58 General Agreement on Tariffs and Trade 1994, 15 April 1994, Marrakesh Agreement Establishing the World Trade Organization, Annex 1A, 1867 UNTS 187 [GATT].

umbrella treaty – as well as in the Agreement on Technical Barriers to Trade (TBT Agreement),[59] the Agreement on Sanitary and Phytosanitary Measures (SPS Agreement)[60] and the Agreement on Trade-Related Aspects of Intellectual Property Rights (TRIPS Agreement).[61]

WTO Instrument	National Treatment	MFN Treatment	Exceptions
GATT 1994	Art. III	Art. I	Art. XX
TBT Agreement	Art. 2.1	Arts. 2.1; 5.1.1; para. 3 Annex D	None
SPS Agreement	Arts. 2.3 and 5.5	Art. 6	Art. 2.4
TRIPS Agreement	Art. 3	Art. 4	Arts. 13, 17 and 30

Figure 4: Legal Principles of WTO Law and their analogue provisions in the relevant WTO Provisions.

Source: Author

The table above illustrates the relationship of the GATT provisions in which the principles of national treatment, most-favoured nation treatment and exceptions are laid out, as well as the analogue provisions in relevant WTO instruments. The following section, although not exhaustive, aims at highlighting the most important aspects of these fundamental WTO principles in relation to the TBT, the SPS and the TRIPS Agreement.

59 Agreement on Technical Barriers to Trade, 1 January 1995, Marrakesh Agreement Establishing the World Trade Organisation, Annex 1A, 1868 UNTS 120 [TBT Agreement].

60 Agreement on Sanitary and Phytosanitary Measures, 1 January 1995, Marrakesh Agreements Establishing the World Trade Organisation, Annex 1A, 1867 UNTS 493 [SPS Agreement].

61 Agreement on Trade-Related Aspects of Intellectual Property Rights, 1 January 1995, Marrakesh Agreement Establishing the World Trade Organisation, Annex 1C, 1869 UNTS 299 [TRIPS Agreement].

1.3.1 National Treatment

Article III GATT imposes upon Members the duty to accord nationals of other Members any treatment that it is not less favourable than that accorded to its own nationals.[62] Upon access to a given market, goods must be treated no less favourably than like products of national origin. In other words, discrimination against foreign products is prohibited.[63] The national treatment prohibition in GATT thus aims at avoiding protectionism in the application of domestic regulatory measures, which extends to fiscal and non-fiscal measures.[64] It also aims at requiring equality of competitive conditions and protecting expectations of equal competitive relationships.[65]

The TBT Agreement establishes in its Article 2.1 that products imported from any Member shall be treated no less favourably than the like products of national origin and the like products originating in any other country. As it was recently addressed by the WTO Dispute Settlement bodies,[66] the national treatment obligation imposed by the TBT Agreement contains three elements: the measure must be a technical regulation, the imported and domestic products at issue are like

62 Subject to certain exemptions and limitations; Trebilcock *et al.*, pp. 136–171.

63 GATT, *Italian Discrimination Against Agricultural Machinery* (Italy – Agricultural Machinery), Decision of 15 July 1958, L/833 – 7S/60, para. 11; GATT, *United States – Section 337 of the Tariff Act of 1930* (US – Section 337), Decision of 16 January 1980, L/6439 – 36S/345, para. 5.10.

64 WTO Appellate Body Report, *Japan – Taxes on Alcoholic Beverages*, 4 October 1996, WT/DS8/AB/R, WT/DS10/AB/R, WT/DS11/AB/R, p. 16 [*Japan – Alcoholic Beverages II*]; Petros Mavroidis, Trade in Goods, Oxford University Press 2007, p. 194.

65 WTO Appellate Body Report, *Korea – Taxes on Alcoholic Beverages*, 18 January 1999, WT/DS84/AB/R, para. 120; WTO Appellate Body Report, *Canada – Certain Measures Concering Periodicals*, 30 June 1997, WT/DS31/AB/R, para. 464; WTO Panel Report, *Argentina – Measures Affecting the Export of Bovine Hides and the Import of Finished Leather* (Argentina – Hides and Leather), 19 December 2000, WT/DS155/R, para. 11.182.

66 WTO Appellate Body, *United States – Measures Affecting the Production and Sale of Clove Cigarettes*, 4 April 2012, WT/DS406/AB/R, para. 87 [*US – Clove Cigarettes*].

products and the treatment accorded to the imported product is no less favourable than that accorded to like domestic products.[67]

Equally, the SPS Agreement imposes in its Articles 2.3 and 5.5 a prohibition of discrimination between countries where identical or similar conditions prevail.[68] Unlike other instruments, however, the national treatment principle in the SPS Agreement has been interpreted as to also prohibit discrimination between different products.[69] The elements of the SPS Agreement that must be fulfilled for the principle of national treatment not to be violated are: the existence of distinctions at appropriate levels of protection in different situations; the existence of arbitrary or unjustifiable distinctions at appropriate levels of protection; and the existence of discrimination or a disguised restriction on international trade.[70]

National Treatment also holds true for TRIPS, albeit with slight differences in the wording. For a measure to be consistent with Article 3 TRIPS, it has to fulfil two requirements: first, the measure must apply with regard to the protection of intellectual property; and second, Members must not accord nationals of other Members any treatment less favourable than that accorded to its own nationals.[71] Furthermore, this provision combines the elements of national treatment provided in pre-existing intellectual property agreements and GATT, such as those found in the Paris

67 WTO Appellate Body, *United States – Measures Concerning the Importation, Marketing and Sale of Tuna and Tuna Products*, 16 May 2012, WT/DS381/AB/R, para. 229 [*US – Tuna II (Mexico)*]; *US – Clove Cigarettes*, para. 87; see *infra*, Chapter 4 on Food Quality Standards as Technical Barriers to Trade.

68 See *infra*, Chapter 6 on Food Safety Standards as Sanitary and Phytosanitary Measures.

69 WTO Appellate Body, *Australia – Measures Affecting the Importation of Salmon*, 20 October 1998, WT/DS18/AB/R, para. 252 [*Australia – Salmon*].

70 *Australia – Salmon*, paras. 227, 234, 237.

71 WTO Appellate Body Report, *United States – Section 211 Omnibus Appropriations Act of 1998*, 2 January 2001, WT/DS176/AB/R, paras. 233–234, 244 [US – Section 211]; WTO Panel Report, *European Communities – Protection of Trademarks and Geographical Indications for Agricultural Products and Foodstuffs (Australia)*, 15 March 2005, WT/DS290/R, paras. 7.89–7.425 [*EC – Trademarks (Australia)*]; WTO Panel Report, *European Communities – Protection of Trademarks and Geographical Indications for Agricultural Products and Foodstuffs (United States)*, 15 March 2005, WT/DS174/R, paras. 7.38–7.499 [*EC – Trademarks]*; see *infra*, Chapter 5 on Food Labelling Standards and Trademark Law.

Convention for the Protection of Industrial Property (Paris Convention),[72] the Berne Convention for the Protection of Literary and Artistic Works (Berne Convention)[73] and the WIPO Treaty on Intellectual Property in respect of Integrated Circuits (IPIC Treaty).[74]

1.3.2 Most-Favoured Nation Treatment

The Most-Favoured Nation Treatment (MFN) found in Article I GATT states that any advantage, favour, privilege or immunity granted by a Member to the nationals of any other country, irrespective of their WTO membership, shall be accorded immediately and unconditionally to the nationals of all other Members.[75] The MFN Treatment is a cornerstone of the GATT and thus one of the essential pillars of the WTO system.[76] Like products must always be treated in the same manner.[77] Its principal purpose it to ensure equality of opportunity to import from, or export to all WTO members, while treating all like products equally, irrespective of their origin.[78] Article I:1 GATT establishes a consistency test with three elements: the measure must confer a trade advantage;[79]

72 Art. 2 of the Paris Convention for the Protection of Industrial Property, 20 March 1883, UNTS 305 [Paris Convention].

73 Art. 5 of the Berne Convention for the Protection of Literary and Artistic Works, 9 September 1886 [Berne Convention].

74 Art. 5 of the WIPO Treaty on Intellectual Property in Respect of Integrated Circuits, 26 May 1989 [IPIC Treaty].

75 Subject to certain exemptions and limitations; Trebilcock *et al.*, pp. 54–82.

76 WTO Appellate Body, *European Communities – Conditions for the Granting of Tariff Preferences to Developing Countries* (EC – Tariff Preferences), 7 April 2004, WT/DS246/AB/R, para. 101; *US – Section 211*, para. 297.

77 WTO Appellate Body Report, *European Communities – Regime for the Importation, Sale and Distribution of Bananas*, 9 September 1997, WT/DS27/AB/R, paras. 190–191 [*EC – Bananas III*].

78 *EC – Bananas III*, para. 190.

79 GATT, *United States Denial of Most-Favoured Nation Treatment as to Non-Rubber Footwear from Brazil*, Decision of 10 January 1992, DS18/R – 39S/128, para. 6.8; GATT, *Unites States Customer User Fee*, Decision of 25 November 1987, L/6264 – 35S/245, para. 122.

the products concerned are like products;[80] and the advantage at issue must be granted immediately and unconditionally to all like products concerned.[81]

As with the national treatment obligation, the MFN treatment is laid out in Article 2.1 (for technical regulations), paragraph D Annex 3 (for standards) and Article 5.1.1 (for conformity assessment procedures) of the TBT Agreement.[82] The SPS Agreement codifies the MFN principle in its Article 6.[83] Similarly, TRIPS contains an analogue provision in its Article 4, related to the specificity of intellectual property.[84]

1.3.3 The Concept of Like Products

An imported product is discriminated in the sense of MFN Treatment and National Treatment if there is a similar domestic product that is treated differently.[85] Thus, the similarity requirement is essential to establish discrimination. Although the concept of likeness is not defined by the GATT, it can be determined on a case-by-case basis under the following criteria: the end-use of a product in a given market, consumers' preferences and the products' properties, nature and quality.[86] It may also involve an examination of evidence relating to the competitive relationship between

80 GATT, *Spain Tariff Treatment on Unroasted Coffee*, Decision of 27 April 1981, L/5135 – 28S/102, para. 4.6–4.7; GATT, *EEC Measures on Animal Feed Proteins*, Decision of 2 December 1977, L/4599 – 25S/49, para. 4.2.

81 GATT, *Belgium Family Allowances*, Decision of 6 November 1952, G/32 – 1S/59, para. 3; WTO Panel Report, *Indonesia – Certain Measures Affecting the Automobile Industry*, 2 July 1998, WT/DS54/55/59/64/R, para. 14.146 [*Indonesia – Autos*].

82 *Cf.* Arkady Kudryavtsev, 'The TBT Agreement in Context' in: Tracey Epps/ Michael Trebilcock, Research Handbook of the WTO and Technical Barriers to Trade, Edward Elgar Publishing 2013, pp. 17–80, p. 55; see *infra*, Chapter 4 on Food Quality Standards as Technical Barriers to Trade.

83 *Australia – Salmon*, para. 110; see *infra*, Chapter 6 on Food Safety Standards as Sanitary and Phytosanitary Measures.

84 *US – Section 211*, paras. 308–318; *EC – Trademarks*, paras. 7.689–7.729; see *infra*, Chapter 5 on Food Labelling Standards and Trademark Law.

85 Art. I:1 and Art. III:2, first sentence, GATT.

86 *US – Section 211*, para. 20; WTO Appellate Body Report, *European Commission – Measures Affecting Asbestos and Asbestos-Containing Products*, 5 April 2001, WT/DS135/AB/R, para. 145 [*EC – Asbestos*].

products in a given market.[87] Therefore, it is generally accepted that like products have different meanings under different circumstances.[88] Although it has originated a considerable amount of WTO jurisprudence, the likeness standard is far from being a settled issue and its status remains disputed to date.[89]

1.3.4 General Exceptions

An inconsistency with the provisions on National Treatment or MFN Treatment may still be compliant with WTO law if the measure at stake falls within the exceptions provided therein. Article XX GATT allows for the protection of important economic societal values, such as public morals, human, animal and plant life, or health.[90] However, the exceptions from obligations arising from other GATT provisions are limited and conditional.[91] In this sense, a balance of interests between affirmative commitments and policy considerations must be struck on a case-by-case basis.[92]

Despite the judicial precedent set by the WTO Appellate Body[93] in applying a wide margin of interpretation to exceptions, the nature of the measure remains the determinant factor in assessing whether it will fall

87 *EC – Asbestos*, para. 91–92; WTO Appellate Body Report, *Korea – Measures Affecting the Importation of Fresh, Chilled and Frozen Beef*, 10 January 2001, WT/DS161/AB/R, para. 144 [Korea – Frozen Beef].

88 *Japan – Alcoholic Beverages II*, para. 114.

89 *US – Clove Cigarettes*, para. 120; Lester *et al.*, p. 320.

90 For an in-depth analysis of the GATT General Exceptions see *generally*: Peter van den Bossche, The Law and Policy of the World Trade Organization: Text, Cases and Materials, Cambridge University Press 2005, p. 615 *et seq.* [Van den Bossche].

91 GATT, *United States Section 337 of the Tariff Act of 1939*, Decision of 7 November 1989, L/6439, BISD36S/345.

92 WTO Appellate Body Report, *United States – Standards for Reformulated and Conventional Gasoline*, 29 April 1996, WT/DS2/AB/R, paras. 16–17 [*US – Gasoline*].

93 For a detailed description of the functioning of the WTO Dispute Settlement System and TRIPS *see*: Frederick Abbott, 'WTO Dispute Settlement and the Agreement on Trade-Related Aspects of Intellectual Property Rights' in: Ernst-Ulrich Petersmann, International Trade Law and the GATT/WTO Dispute Settlement System, Kluwer Law International 1997, pp. 413–437.

within the category of justified exceptions to substantive obligations[94] In particular, it must be noted here that a GATT-inconsistent measure may be justified under Article XX(d) GATT if it is necessary to ensure compliance with domestic legislation. A two-tier test will then be applied. First, the aim of the measure must be to secure compliance with domestic laws that are not inconsistent with GATT provisions. And second, the measure must be necessary to ensure compliance.[95]

Unlike the GATT, the TBT Agreement does not provide for a rule containing general exceptions.

The SPS Agreement however, provides in its Article 2.4 that sanitary and phytosanitary measures in compliance with the SPS Agreement are presumed to be compliant with the obligations under the GATT.[96] In other words, the exceptions under the SPS Agreement do not require an inconsistency with its other provisions, as it would be the case with a general exception under Article XX of the GATT.[97]

The TRIPS Agreement has also been vested with exceptions throughout. This is so due to the fact that the rights falling under its scope of protection are of a different nature. It follows that the exceptions and limitations to copyright are found in Article 13,[98] whereas the exceptions to the patent rights conferred are provided for in Article 30 of the TRIPS Agreement.[99] For justified exceptions to rights conferred to trademark holders, the TRIPS Agreement offers a provision in Article 17.[100]

94 WTO Appellate Body Report, *United States – Import Prohibition of Certain Shrimp and Shrimp Products*, 12 October 1998, WT/DS58/AB/R, para. 121 [*US – Shrimps*].

95 *Korea – Frozen Beef*, para. 157.

96 See *infra*, Chapter 6 on Food Safety Standards and Sanitary and Phytosanitary Measures.

97 WTO Panel Report, *European Communities Measures Concerning Meat and Meat Products (Hormones)*, Complaint by Canada, 29 March 1989, WT/DS48/R/CAN, para. 8.41 [*EC – Hormones*].

98 For an analysis of copyright exceptions in Article 13 TRIPS *see*: WTO Panel Report, *United States – Section 110(5) of the US Copyright Act*, 15 June 2000, WT/DS160/R.

99 For an analysis of patent exceptions in Art. 30 TRIPS *see*: WTO Panel Report, *Canada – Patent Protection of Pharmaceutical Products*, 17 March 2000, WT/DS114/R [*Canada – Pharmaceuticals*].

100 See *infra*, Chapter 5 on Food Labelling Standards and Trademark Law.

1.4 Conclusion

In the light of recent changes in the dynamics governing world food markets, the last decades have seen a paradigm shift in the legal architecture governing trade in food. With the creation of the WTO, and the changing trends in food production and distribution as a backdrop, the challenges posed by new forms of global food governance are evident. In addition, the formation of traditional, binding treaty rules stagnated in favor of informal, soft rules.[101] Indeed, new forms of global food governance are being laid down by both state and non-state actors and are visible through regulations, standards, guidelines and recommendations of the most varied nature. These complex set of rules invariably affect the free flow of international trade in foodstuffs and thus, the reduction of potential trade-distorting effects is paramount to their successful implementation.

Chapter 1 laid down the legal and economic foundations upon which the present research is built. Based on findings from the political sciences, section II examined the different available definitions of good governance[102] to later address the essential elements present in the governance of food.[103] It concluded that, for the purposes of this thesis, global food governance refers to a complex set of private and public rules, including regulations and standards, laid down by international institutions and private bodies that go beyond the realm of public policy in order to attain the ultimate common good.

Section III presented the relevant economic theories of international trade. It first addressed whether market access constitutes the ultimate goal of regulation by implementing the theory of competitive advantage. It then turned to examine the impact of market failures, particularly information asymmetry, in the creation of trade rules. After the establishment of the WTO and with a shift towards deep integration trade rules aiming at harmonisation, this section highlighted the relevance of the current

101 Also called 'new forms of cooperation': JOOST PAUWELYN, 'Rule-Based Trade 2.0? The Rise of Informal Rules and International Standards and How They May Outcompete WTO Treaties' (2014) 14 Journal of International Economic Law, pp. 1–13, p. 2.

102 See Figure 2, Definition of Good Governance.

103 See Figure 3, Elements of Food Governance.

multilateral trading system in solving disputes arising out of divergent standards.

The last section summarised the most relevant legal principles of WTO law for food standardisation. National Treatment, MFN Treatment, the concept of like products and general exceptions constitute the foundations of all WTO instruments, including the TBT Agreement, the SPS Agreement and the TRIPS Agreement.[104]

As will be shown, these WTO instruments play a fundamental role in the creation of new forms of food governance. Hence, the following chapter will examine the importance of food standards in international trade law.

104 See Figure 4, Relevant WTO Principles and their analogue provisions.

2. The Importance of Food Standards in International Trade Law

2.1 Introduction

2.1.1 The Role of Standards

Standards are found in all realms of human activity in order to specify the characteristics of a product or its manufacture. While doing this, they fulfill a range of functions, such as lowering risks, increasing trust and facilitating predictability in a given market.[105] Hence, standard setting aims at providing a rational process to solve technical problems, based on science and governance.[106] Standards reduce information costs for market players, which in turn allow for a more efficient functioning of the market.[107] In particular, the harmonisation of the wide variety of food standards appears essential in facilitating the global food-sourcing trend.[108] International trade agreements have been influencing these recent developments since the establishment of the WTO. As traditional market access barriers are dismantled, non-tariff measures – such as sanitary and phytosanitary measures and technical regulations – seem

105 SMITH, para. 25.

106 THOMAS LOYA/JOHN BOLI, 'Standardization in the World Policy: Technical Rationality over Power' in: JOHN BOLI/GEORGE THOMAS (eds), Constructing World Culture, Stanford University Press 1999, pp. 169–197, p. 193.

107 STEVE CHARNOVITZ, 'International Standards and the WTO', The George Washington University Law School Public Law and Legal Theory Working Paper Nr. 133, May 2002, p. 12.

108 This chapter is partly based on previously published work, see: MARIELA MAIDANA-ELETTI, 'International Food Standards and WTO Law', (2014) 19 (2) Deakin Law Review, pp. 217–241 [MAIDANA-ELETTI, International Food Standards]. On the proliferation of food standards in the private sector *see*: LINDA FULPONI, 'Private Voluntary Standards in the Food System: The Perspective of Major Food Retailers in OECD Countries' (2006) 31 Food Policy, pp. 1–13.

to provide a tool for potential non-compliance with international law, thus calling for better forms of governance.

The rationale behind this statement is found in the WTO Agreements, particularly in the TBT Agreement, the SPS Agreement and the TRIPS Agreement. These WTO instruments, to varying extents, encourage the design and adoption of international standards by imposing their use as a basis for regulation. This circumstance in turn creates a presumption of compliance with WTO rules that ultimately facilitate international trade. International standards thus act as a benchmark for better forms of governance while avoiding the adoption of trade-distorting measures and promoting harmonisation. This statement holds particularly true for trade in foodstuffs, whereas compliance with food safety and quality standards will ultimately determine market access.

As put forward in the previous chapter, the concept of 'food standard' followed in this thesis differs from the definition of standard given by the TBT Agreement[109] in that it encompasses not only voluntary documents, but also mandatory rules. Along the same line as the TBT Agreement however, the term as used in this thesis does not differentiate between public or private standards more than it is necessary to recognise the legal framework the standard-setting body is embedded in. Hence, food standards shall be here understood as all regulations, rules, guidelines and recommendations applicable to trade in foodstuffs.

2.1.2 The Concept of International Standards

The TBT Agreement recognises the importance of international standards for international trade and thus imposes upon Members the obligation to use international standards as the foundation for regulatory practices, while leaving a margin of discretion as to the choice of measure and its use.[110] The relevant provision is found in Article 2.4 of the TBT Agreement:

109 Annex 1 of the TBT Agreement; see also *infra*, Chapter 4 on Food Quality Standards.

110 Erik Wijkstrom/Devin Mcdaniels, 'International Standards and the WTO TBT Agreement: Improving Governance for Regulatory Alignment' World Trade Organization, Economic Research and Statistics Division, Staff Working Paper ERSD, 25 April 2013, p. 3 [Wijkstrom/Mcdaniels].

> [w]here technical regulations are required and relevant international standards exist or their completion is imminent, Members shall use them, or the relevant parts of them, as a basis for their technical regulations except when such international standards or relevant parts would be an ineffective or inappropriate means for the fulfillment of the legitimate objectives pursued, for instance because of fundamental climatic or geographical factors or fundamental technological problems.[111]

This provision was called upon in four disputes that have been adjudicated in the WTO Dispute Settlement.[112] Based on this jurisprudence, a three-step analysis was established to determine compliance with Article 2.4 of the TBT Agreement.[113]

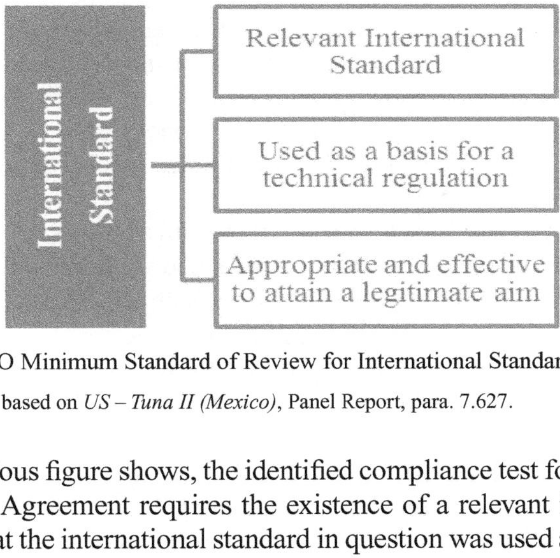

Figure 5: WTO Minimum Standard of Review for International Standards.

Source: Author, based on *US – Tuna II (Mexico)*, Panel Report, para. 7.627.

As the previous figure shows, the identified compliance test for Article 2.4 of the TBT Agreement requires the existence of a relevant international standard, that the international standard in question was used as a basis for

111 Art. 2.4 TBT Agreement.

112 *US – Tuna II (Mexico)*; WTO Panel Report, *European Communities – Trade Definition of Sardines*, 29 May 2002, WT/DS231/R [*EC – Sardines,* Panel Report]; WTO Appellate Body, EC – Sardines, 26 September 2002, WT/DS231/AB/R [*EC – Sardines*]; *US – Clove Cigarettes*; WTO Appellate Body, *United States Certain Country of Origin Labelling (COOL) Requirements*, 29 June 2012, WT/DS384/386/AB/R [*US – COOL*].

113 *US – Tuna II (Mexico)*, para. 7.627.

a technical regulation, and that the international standard in question is an effective or appropriate means for the fulfillment of the legitimate objectives pursued. These steps will be discussed in detail as follows.

2.2 What is a Relevant International Standard?

The WTO Appellate Body first addressed the notion of international relevant standards in *EC – Sardines*. In that case, a European regulation controlling the labelling and marketing requirements of preserved sardines was challenged by Peru under Article 2.4 of the TBT Agreement. This measure allowed for the marketing and labelling of products prepared from a specific species of sardines, the European Sardina Pichardus, to the exclusion of products prepared from other species of sardines, such as the Peruvian Sardinops Sagax.

The WTO Appellate Body based its findings on an analysis of the relevance of an international standard for canned sardines and sardine-type products in the light of the standard Codex Stan 94, drafted by the Codex Alimentarius Commission.[114] Concurring with the conclusion reached by the WTO Panel Report,[115] the Appellate Body agreed that the ordinary meaning of the term 'relevant' is 'bearing upon or relating to the matter in hand; pertinent'.[116] It followed that in the case at hand, for Codex Stan 94 to be a relevant international standard, it had to bear upon, relate to, or be pertinent to the EC regulation challenged.[117] Because the challenged measure dealt with the same product as the Codex Stan 94 and included the provisions set out in the Codex Stan 94, it was found that the CAC

114 Codex Alimentarius Commission [CAC] as established by the Joint FAO/WHO Conference on Food Standards, Report Session, 1 to 5 October 1962, Geneva, ALINORM 62/8 [Joint FAO/WHO Food Standards Conference].

115 *EC – Sardines*, Panel Report, para. 7.68, quoting Webster's New World Dictionary, William Collins & World Publishing Co., Inc. 1976, p. 1199.

116 *EC – Sardines*, para. 231–232.

117 *EC – Sardines*, Panel Report, para. 7.68.

standard in question provided sufficient basis to be considered a 'relevant international standard' in that case.[118]

Relevant Standard *EC – Sardines*	**International Standard** *US – Tuna II (Mexico)*
A standard is relevant if it is: • Bearing upon; • Relating to the matter; • Pertinent.	A standard is international if it is designed by a body with: • Recognized activities in standardization • Open membership to WTO members

Figure 6: WTO Threshold for Relevant Standards.

Source: Author

As illustrated in the table above, the reasoning developed *in EC – Sardines* was upheld in *US – Tuna II (Mexico)*, where Mexico challenged US regulation establishing the conditions for use of a 'dolphin-safe' label on tuna products. The Appellate Body was called upon to assess whether the dolphin-safe definition and certification standards defined by the Agreement on International Dolphin Conservation Program (AIDCO), which establish dolphin mortality limits, specific fishing techniques and fishing gear to reduce dolphin by-catch, constituted a relevant international standard. In this case, however, the 'relevant international standard' for the purposes of the TBT Agreement was identified in accordance with the characteristics of the standard-setting body. Based on an interpretation of the definitions set out in Annex 1 of the TBT Agreement and the ISO/IEC Guide 2:1991, the Appellate Body stated that an international standardising body is 'a body that has recognised activities in standardisation and whose membership is open to the relevant bodies of all WTO Members'.[119] It further elaborated on the concept of membership openness, setting out three requirements: no restrictions on membership by WTO members;[120] automatic accession;[121] and to be open at all stages of standard development.[122]

118 *EC – Sardines*, Panel Report, para. 7.69.
119 *US – Tuna II (Mexico)*, para. 359.
120 *US – Tuna II (Mexico)*, para. 364.
121 *US – Tuna II (Mexico)*, para. 386.
122 *US – Tuna II (Mexico)*, para. 374.

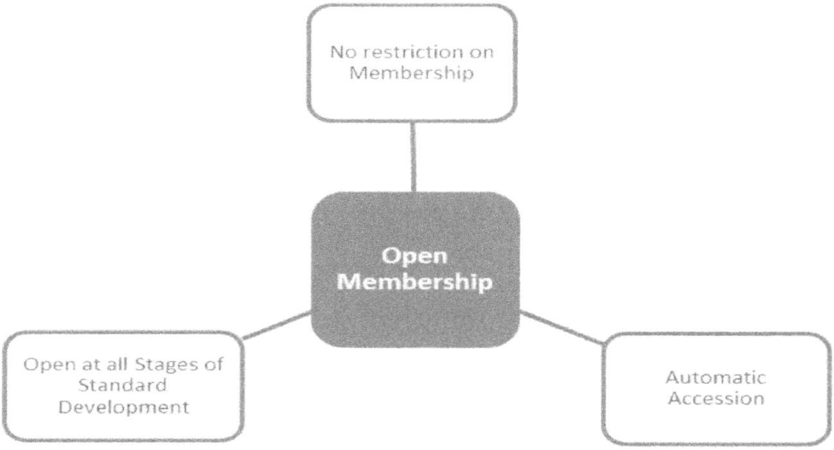

Figure 7: WTO Open Membership Test.

Source: Author

The Appellate Body concluded that AIDCO standards could not be deemed as 'relevant international standards' for the purposes of Article 2.4 of the TBT Agreement, because the organisation did not qualify as an 'international standardisation body' due to its lack of membership openness to all relevant WTO Members.[123]

The most recent case addressing the importance of the relevant international standard was *US – Clove Cigarettes*. In this case, Indonesia challenged a US measure banning the production and sale of cigarettes with flavours other than tobacco or menthol. Although no challenge was brought under Article 2.4 of the TBT Agreement,[124] both the Panel and the Appellate Body stated that it was aware of international standards to curb smoking within the WHO Framework Convention on Tobacco

123 Accession was only by invitation, which in turn had to be extended by consensus among members.

124 Panel Report, *US – Clove Cigarettes*, para. 7.496; Appellate Body Report, *US – Clove Cigarettes*, para. 235.

Control.[125] The fact that the Panel decided to mention its awareness of international standardisation tendencies, even though no formal challenge had been brought against a measure based on an international standard, demonstrates once again the relevance of the standardisation process on the global level.

2.3 International Standard as a Basis for Regulation

The question of whether a relevant international standard has been used as a basis for regulation was also addressed in *EC – Sardines*. In that case, the Appellate Body agreed with the Panel Report that an international standard is used 'as a basis for'[126] a technical regulation when it is used as a principal constituent or fundamental principle in enacting that technical regulation. It further stated that there must be a 'very strong and very close relationship'[127] between the challenged measure and the invoked international standard for the latter to constitute a basis for the former.

International Standard used as a Basis for Regulation		
principal constituent or fundamental principle	very strong and very close relationship	lack of contradiction between the standard and the regulation

Figure 8: WTO Threshold for Regulations based on International Standards.

Source: Author

As illustrated in the figure above, the Appellate Body continued to lay down the minimum standard of connection between the measure and

125 WHO Framework Convention on Tobacco Control, 21 May 2003, UNTS. 2302, 166 [WHO FCTC].

126 *EC – Sardines*, paras. 240–245.

127 *EC – Sardines*, para. 243.

the standard in the lack of contradiction between them. In the words used by the Appellate Body:

> [...] it can certainly be said – at a minimum – that something cannot be considered as a "basis" for something else if the two are contradictory. Therefore, under Article 2.4, if the technical regulation and the international standard contradict each other, it cannot properly be concluded that the international standard has been used "as a basis for" the technical regulation.[128]

While construing this interpretation, the Appellate Body deemed it relevant to refer to its approach in interpreting the term 'based on' in the context of Article 3.1 of the SPS Agreement.[129] This provision establishes a presumption of compliance with the SPS Agreement, whereas the challenged measure is based on international (food) standards, designed and adopted by the CAC.[130]

Following this line, the TBT Agreement and its interpretative jurisprudence lend themselves to establish a presumption of compliance, whereby technical regulations are presumed not to be trade-distorting if adopted in accordance with a relevant international standard.[131] In contrast to the SPS Agreement, however, where reference is made to specific standard-setting bodies, the TBT Agreement offers a larger margin of discretion in choosing the relevant international standardisation body and their standards as a basis for a WTO compliant measure.

2.4 Effectiveness and Appropriateness of Attaining a Legitimate Aim

The implicit obligations of WTO Members to base their TBT measures on relevant international standards can only be avoided in cases where

128 *EC – Sardines*, para. 248.

129 *EC – Sardines*, para. 242; see *infra*, Chapter 6 on Food Safety Standards as Sanitary and Phytosanitary Measures.

130 See *infra*, Chapter 3 on Food Standard-Setting Organisations.

131 WIJKSTROM/MCDANIELS, p. 14.

their use would lead to an inappropriate or ineffective level of protection for the fulfillment of their legitimate objectives.

2.4.1 Effectiveness and Appropriateness

The Appellate Body upheld the interpretation given by the Panel in *EC – Sardines*, whereby the term 'ineffective' refers to something that does not have the function of accomplishing, having a result or bringing to bear; and the term 'inappropriate' refers to something which is not specially suitable, proper or fitting to achieve a legitimate objective.[132] The Appellate Body further agreed on the statement by the Panel that these two terms have different meanings, stating that 'it is conceptually possible that a measure could be effective but inappropriate, or appropriate but ineffective'.[133] In other words, both requirements must be cumulatively fulfilled for a measure to be compliant with Article 2.4 of the TBT Agreement. Later, the Panel Report on *US – Tuna II (Mexico)* recalled both this statement while establishing that Mexico bear the burden of showing that the AIDCP standard is both effective and appropriate.[134]

2.4.2 Legitimate Objectives

In *US – COOL*, the Appellate Body defined the concept of 'legitimate objectives' while assessing whether certain US requirements for labelling meat products were in compliance with TBT obligations. It acknowledged the legitimacy of a US measure requiring the disclosure of country of origin information for the labelling of meat products, intended to inform consumers 'on the countries in which the livestock from which the meat they purchase is produces were born, raised and slaughtered.'[135] However, the costs associated with the implementation of that measure, which did not necessarily translate in additional information being provided to consumers, would *de facto* lead to an exclusive use

132 *EC – Sardines*, para. 7.116.
133 *EC – Sardines*, Panel Report, para. 289.
134 *US – Tuna II (Mexico)*, para. 7.725.
135 *US – COOL*, paras. 449–453.

of domestic livestock by US producers and 'thus has a detrimental impact on the competitive opportunities of imported livestock'.[136] Hence, a balanced approach is necessary to guarantee the souvereign right of WTO members to adopt domestic measures against their right to trade in other WTO member's market.

2.5 Conclusion

Although voluntary in nature, food standards can be vested of a legally binding character by reference to the presumption of compliance implicit in the WTO Agreements. The concept of international standard captured by the TBT Agreement provides a legal base to assess the conformity of domestic food measures with WTO members' international law obligations. In particular, Article 2.4 of the TBT Agreement and its judicial interpretations offer a benchmark against which the legality of *prima facie* protectionist measures can be tested.[137]

Based on four leading cases, the WTO Appellate Body first developed a two-tier test that conceptualises 'relevant international standards' as those pertinent standards designed by recognised standardisation bodies with open membership for WTO members,[138] followed by a second step in the minimum standard of review, the use of an international standard as a basis for regulation.[139] A three-tier subtest was identified, according to which it must first be apparent that the international standard was used as a principal constituent or fundamental principle in enacting that technical regulation and secondly, there must be a very strong and close relationship between the standard invoked and the regulation enacted. Finally, there must be a lack of contradiction between the former and the latter. Significantly, the last aspect developed by the WTO

136 *US – COOL*, para. 349.

137 See *supra* Figure 5: WTO Minimum Standard of Review for International Standards.

138 See *supra* Figure 6: WTO Threshold for Relevant Standards.

139 See *supra* Figure 8: WTO Threshold for Regulations based on International Standards.

Appellate Body in determining conformity with Article 2.4 of the TBT Agreement is found in an *argumentum e contrario*, according to which WTO Members have a right not to base their regulations on relevant international standards in cases when its use would lead to an inappropriate or ineffective level of protection for the fulfillment of its legitimate objectives.

Although the definition of international standard is still far from precise, the interpretative path developed by the WTO Appellate Body offers an increased certainty as to the extents to which the relevant stakeholders and governments may rely on voluntary food standards in order to comply with international law obligations. It remains to be seen whether the TBT Agreement provides enough legal flexibility to adapt to the increasing role played by standard-setting bodies embedded in private law.

The next chapter will address the fundamental role played by relevant standardisation bodies recognised under WTO law. While doing so, it will illustrate the procedural mechanisms followed on the international and domestic levels.

3. Food Standard-Setting Organisations

3.1 Introduction

The previous chapter showed that standard-setting organisations with international dimensions play a fundamental role in assessing the WTO compatibility of domestic regulation. This also holds true for food safety and quality standards. While the Codex Alimentarius Commission (CAC) is the leading standard-setting body for food safety, the International Organisation for Standardization (ISO), with its comprehensive set of standards, has also acquired an important role in aspects related to food quality. Although there exist other relevant standard-setting organisations with their own internal dispute settlement mechanisms[140] for animal health and zoonoses[141] as well as for plant health,[142] this chapter will not deal with them.[143]

The various obligations of WTO members to base their domestic measures in relevant international standards justify an analysis in the following sections. In spite of their voluntary nature, the standards designed by relevant international standard-setting bodies have therefore received a higher and sometimes disputed legal status. This is due to the explicit inclusion in WTO instruments – as it is the case with

140 MARINA FOLTEA, International Organizations in WTO Dispute Settlement: How Much Sensitivity? Cambridge University Press 2012, p. 157.

141 Such as the International Office of Epizootics, *fr.* International des Epizooties [OIE].

142 Such as the International Plant Protection Convention [IPPC].

143 For a short overview of the IPPC and the OIE *see*: TERENCE STEWART/DAVID JOHANSEN, 'The SPS Agreement of the World Trade Organisation and Interntional Organisations: The Roles of the Codex Alimentarious Commission, the International Plant Protection Convention and the International Office of Epizootics' (1998) 26 Syracuse Journal of International Law, pp. 27–54.

the CAC[144] or due to agreement interpretation by the WTO dispute settlement system.[145] Hence, this chapter aims at analysing the legal mechanisms of the CAC and the ISO, addressing their rules of procedure, development and adoption of standards. As a mode of illustrative example and before concluding, this chapter will then analyse the same legal mechanisms of domestic food standard-setting bodies, taking Germany as a case study.

3.2 The Codex Alimentarius Commission

The most influential food standard-setting body at the international level is the Codex Alimentarius Commission (CAC).[146] Its main objective is to adopt international food standards for the protection of public health and the promotion of fair practice in food trade.[147] Unlike the more contemporary WTO instruments, the CAC was established in 1962 by the Joint FAO/WHO Food Standards Programme as their subsidiary body to respond to the increased trade in food.[148] It elaborates on international standards, codes of practice, guidelines and related texts addressing food

144 Annex A to the SPS Agreement.

145 *EC – Sardines*; *US – Tuna II (Mexico)*; see *supra*, Chapter 2 on the Importance of Food Standards in International Trade.

146 This section is partly based on previous published work, *see supra*: MAIDANA-ELETTI, International Food Standards. Other international institutions also devote their work to setting standards in the area of food safety, *e.g.* the Organisation for Economic Cooperation and Development (OECD); see *generally*: GERALD SANDER, 'Codex Alimentarius Commission (CAC)' in: RÜDIGER WOLFRUM (ed), The Max Planck Encyclopedia of Public International Law, Volume II, Oxford University Press 2012, pp. 276–281.

147 JOINT FAO/WHO FOOD STANDARDS PROGRAM; Art. 1(c), (d) and (e) of the Procedural Manual, Codex Alimentarius Commission, Joint FAO/WHO Food Standards Program, 19th ed., Rome 2010 [CAC Procedural Manual].

148 As a subsidiary organ, the CAC depends financially and institutionally on the FAO and the WHO, which in turn impairs its ability to rapidly and effectively adopt standards.

safety and quality to facilitate international trade.[149] For many decades, the legal relevance of adopted CAC standards was dismissed due to their non-binding, merely advisory nature.[150] It was first with the adoption of the WTO Agreements that the Codex Alimentarius was upgraded to a semi-binding status. Both the SPS and the TBT Agreements explicitly refer to CAC standards as a way to sustain a presumption of compliance with food safety rules.

The binding nature of CAC standards has been intensely debated and no consensus has been achieved among legal scholars.[151] The findings of the WTO Appellate Body in *EC – Hormones*[152] explicitly rejected the argument that international standards should be accorded binding force. Fifteen years after these findings, the *de facto* binding nature of CAC standards still continues to be questioned.[153] It has even opened the debate on the legitimacy and transparency of the adoption process within the CAC.[154] In particular, there are questions regarding whether the

149 Codex Alimentarius Commission, Understanding The Codex Alimentarius, 3rd Ed., WHO/FAO, Rome 2006 [CAC, Understanding the Codex]; Codex Alimentarius Commission, This is Codex Alimentarius, 1995.

150 Prior to the adoption of the SPS Agreement, CAC standards were only binding when voluntarily transposed into national legislation and thus, they remained untouched by national or international political interests. See *generally*: Matthias Herdegen, 'Biotechnology and Regulatory Risk Assessment' in: George Bermann/Matthias Herdegen/Peter Lindseth (eds), Transatlantic Regulatory Cooperation: Legal Problems and Political Prospects, Oxford University Press 2001, pp. 301–317; Frode Veggeland/Svein Borgen, Changing the Codex: The Role of International Institutions Norwegian Agricultural Economics Research Institute, Oslo, January 2002.

151 Rejecting the binding nature of CAC standards *see*: Joanne Scott, 'International Trade and Environmental Governance: Relating Rules (and Standards) in the EU and the WTO' (2004) 15 (2) European Journal of International Law, pp. 307–54; Reinhard Quick/Andreas Blunther, 'Has the Appellate Body erred? An Appraisal and Criticism of the Ruling in the WTO Hormones Case' (1999) Journal of International Economic Law, pp. 603–39.

152 *EC – Hormones*, paras. 162–5.

153 Illustrating the current discussion on the binding force of CAC standards *see*: Marielle Matthee, 'The Codex Alimentarius Commission and its Food Safety Measures in the Light of their New Status' in: Michelle Everson/Ellen Vos (eds), Uncertain Risks Regulated, Routledge Cavendish 2009, pp. 325–329.

154 The legitimacy of the CAC to adopt international standards remains questioned; see *inter alia*: Henrik Horn/Joseph Weiler, 'European Communities – Trade

lengthy adoption process and the rapid development of new technologies affecting food production are rather hindering the harmonisation efforts this institution has been entrusted with.[155]

As shown in recent WTO case law however, concerns about procedural transparency and legitimacy should not distract from the semi-binding nature CAC standards have been vested with. A joint analysis of the EC-Hormones case, which specifically rejected the binding nature of CAC standards in the context of the SPS Agreement, together with the compliance test designed by the Appellate Body in EC-Sardines[156] leads to the conclusion that different WTO agreements may provide sufficient legal flexibilities in their provisions so as to allow CAC standards to create a *prima facie* presumption of compliance with WTO law.

3.2.1 CAC Rules of Procedure

CAC Membership is open to all WHO and FAO Members. It is led by an executive committee, consisting of the Chair of the Commission, three Vice-chairs, Coordinators appointed by the Commission for certain regions or group of countries, and seven members, one each for Africa, Asia, Europe, the Near East, North America, the South-west Pacific, and

---

Description of Sardines: Textualism and its Discontent' in: HENRIK HORN/PETROS MAVROIDIS (eds), The WTO Case Law of 2002, Cambridge University Press 2005, pp. 248–75; SYDNEY SHAPIRO, 'International Trade Agreements, Regulatory Protection and Public Accountability' (2002) 54 (1) Administrative Law Review, pp. 435–457. Likewise, transparency concerns are still being discussed among CAC Members; see *inter alia*: Joint FAO/WHO Food Standards Program, Report of the 22nd Session, 11 to 15 April 2005, Paris, ALINORM 05/28/33A, paras. 98–105; Joint FAO/WHO Food Standards Program, Report of the 19th (extraordinary) Session, 17–21 November 2003, Paris, ALINORM 04/27/33, paras. 40–45.

155 Regretting the increased politicisation of internal mechanisms of standard adoption see: ALBERTO ALEMANNO, Trade in Food: Regulatory and Judicial Approaches in the EC and the WTO, Cameron May 2007, pp. 273–274 [ALEMANNO].

156 Also: *US – Tuna II (Mexico)*; *US – Clove Cigarettes*. See *supra*, Chapter 2 on the Importance of International Standards.

Latin America and the Caribbean. The Executive Committee meets annually as well as before each Commission session.[157]

The CAC Secretariat is based in Rome, at FAO headquarters. It provides administrative support with the organisation of the sessions and the coordination of the work carried out by subsidiary bodies to the Codex.[158] The CAC functions according to its Procedural Manual, which is composed of the Codex Statutes and the Rules of Procedure. The Manual sets up rules for membership, the appointment and responsibilities of officers, the frequency and operation of Codex sessions, voting procedure, and the preparation of records, reports and budget allocations.[159]

Decisions are adopted by consensus, although the Rules of Procedure requires majority of votes. Senior officials appointed by their respective governments form the delegations that represent each Member State, which has one vote. Observers, and those granted observer statues (such as representatives of the industry, consumer associations, and international academic institutes) are allowed to participate in the decision-making process, without a vote.

3.2.2 The Development of CAC Standards

The standards developed by the CAC address processed, semi-processed and raw food. They also contain numerous maximum residue limits for pesticides in foods and animal feed, residue levels for veterinary drugs in foods of animal origin, and acceptable levels of food additives and contaminants.[160] The preparation of these standards takes place in Codex Committees. These Committees are of two types: Commodity Committees and General Subject Committees.

157 CAC, Understanding the Codex, p. 15; Jessica Vapnek/Melvin Spreij, 'Perspectives and Guidelines on Food Legislation: With a New Model Food Law' FAO Legislative Study 97, FAO 2005, p. 30 [Vapnek/Spreij].

158 CAC, Understanding the Codex, p. 19; Vapnek/Spreij, p. 31.

159 CAC, Understanding the Codex, p. 14; Vapnek/Spreij, p. 30.

160 CAC, Understanding the Codex, p. 11; Vapnek/Spreij, p. 31.

Commodity Committees develop vertical standards on food quality. Their subject matter includes fresh fruit and vegetables, processed meat and poultry products. Some of these Committees have already completed their work and are now inactive for an unspecified period of time, while others are kept active to review and align standards with current practice. This in turn has resulted in a loss of prominence for Commodity Committees in favour of horizontal safety standards being developed by the General Subjects Committees.[161] General Subjects Committees develop principles applicable horizontally to all or a specific group of food products, while developing recommendations on consumer health and safety. These Committees generally rely on independent expert advice to design and develop food standards.[162]

3.2.3 The Adoption of CAC Standards

The CAC develops and adopts standards according to its strategic six-year plan, which acts as a benchmark for submitted individual proposals. The strategic plan is reviewed every two years in order to adjust to current demands. The Executive Committee critically reviews new proposals for standards in order to ensure their development within a reasonable period of time based on the requirements and availability of expert scientific advice. The subsequent procedure to develop or renew an existing standard is illustrated below.

161 CAC, Understanding the Codex, pp. 17–18; Vapnek/Spreij, p. 33.
162 CAC, Understanding the Codex, pp. 17–18; Vapnek/Spreij, p. 30.

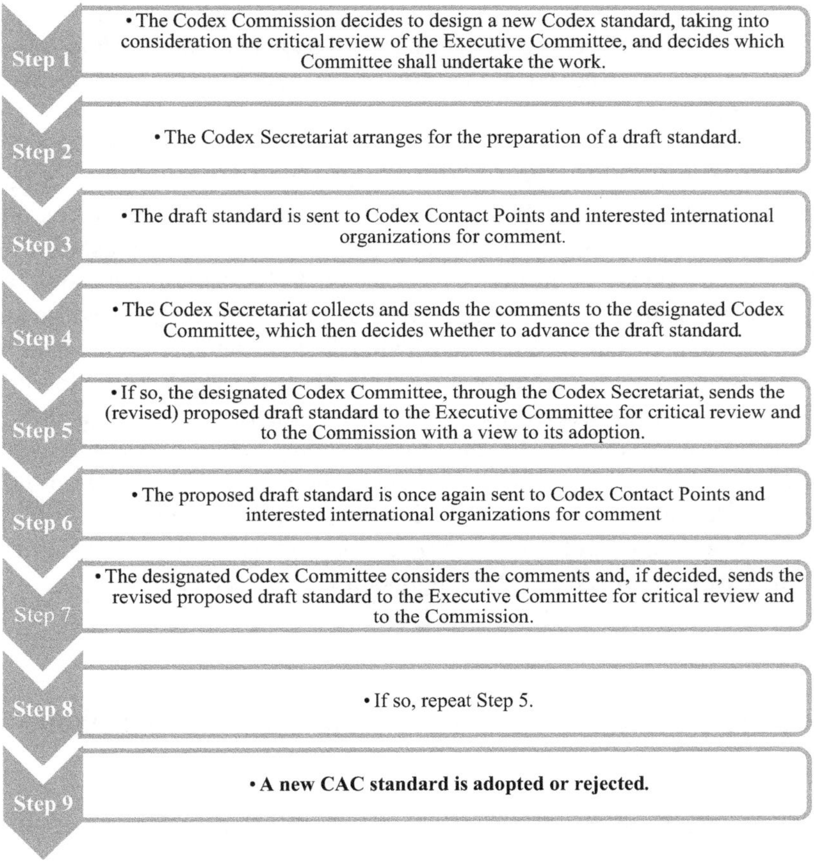

Figure 9: CAC Standard-Setting Procedure.

Source: FAO, Introduction to Codex Alimentarius Commission,[163] revised by the Author.

This decision-making process represents collective policy action and multilateral cooperation through the joint activities of the FAO and WHO, which ultimately aim at attaining high levels of consumer protection, public health and food safety.[164] With a view to making the adoption of

163 FAO, Introduction to Codex Alimentarius Commission, Food Quality and Standards Services, Food and Nutrition Division, Module 4, available at: <http://www.fao.org/docrep/003/x7354e/x7354e04.htm> (last visited: 30 June 2015).

164 WHO, Global Strategy for Food Safety.

Codex standards more inclusive, transparent and, ultimately more effective, a joint FAO/WHO/CAC evaluation was carried out in 2002. As a result of this, the Codex Commission adopted several amendments in its rules of procedure.[165]

The number of international food standards, guidelines and recommendations adopted by the CAC that have been implemented in domestic legislation has dramatically increased. This change is mainly due on one hand to the recognition of the Codex Alimentarius as the main source for food safety standards in the SPS Agreement.[166] On the other hand, the Codex Alimentarius gained importance by being indirectly recognised as an international standard-setting organisation by the TBT Agreement.[167] The resulting reinforcement of legitimacy is tangible. Whereas the first thirty years of the Codex' existence were characterised by the adoption of standards largely implemented in developing countries seeking major access, the last decade saw a significant increase in the Codex' profile among developed countries.[168] Ultimately, it is the promotion of policy cooperation and regulatory harmonisation required to overcome global trade barriers that is the underlying factor of CAC success.[169]

3.3 The International Organization for Standardization

The International Organization for Standardization (ISO) was created during a conference at the Institute of Civil Engineers in London in 1946 to facilitate the international coordination and unification of industrial

165 Joint FAO/WHO Food Standards Program, Report of the 28th Session, 4 to 9 July 2005, Rome, ALINORM 05/28/27.

166 See *infra*, Chapter 6 on Food Safety Standards as Sanitary and Phytosanitary Measures.

167 *EC – Sardines*; see *supra*, Chapter 2 on the Importance of Food Standards in International Trade Law.

168 Michael Livermore, 'Authority and Legitimacy in Global Governance: Deliberation, Institutional Differentiation and the Codex Alimentarius' (2006) 81 New York University Law Review, pp. 766–801.

169 Joint FAO/WHO Food Standards Programme, Report of the 24th Session, 15 November 2000, Geneva, ALINORM 01/23, p. 12.

standards.[170] The ISO was the result of combining two already existing standard-setting organizations:[171] the International Federation of the National Standardizing Associations (ISA)[172] and the United Nations Standards Coordinating Committee (UNSCC).[173] The main objective of the ISO is to promote the development of standardisation worldwide and so facilitate the international exchange of goods.[174]

3.3.1 ISO Membership

Unlike the CAC, the ISO is a non-governmental organisation with members from 162 countries, which draw solely from their respective national standards bodies.[175] Members can delegate their rights and obligations to other organizations, but they remain responsible to the other members.[176] However, membership is limited to one institution (private or public) per country;[177] whichever represents the standardisation practices of that country best. The ISO has three types of membership: full member bodies, correspondent members and subscriber members.

170 Vapnek/Spreij, p. 44.

171 ISO, Friendship Among Equals: Recollection from ISO's First Fifty Years, ISO 1997, p. 15.

172 The International Federation of the National Standardizing Associations (ISA) was created in New York in 1926.

173 The United Nations Standards Coordinating Committee (UNSCC) was created in London in 1944.

174 Art. 2.1 of the ISO Statutes, 17th ed., available at: <http://www.iso.org/iso/statutes.pdf> (last visited: 30 June 2015) [ISO Statutes].

175 Art. 3.3 of the ISO Statutes. The recent modification in ISO membership as per 2012 reflects a much-needed change in internal policy, whereby no bodies other than the national standard bodies may be eligible for ISO membership.

176 ISO Membership Manual, August 2013, available at: <http://www.iso.org/iso/iso_membership_manual_2013.pdf> (last visited: 30 June 2015), p. 7 [ISO Membership Manual].

177 Art. 3.2 of the ISO Statutes.

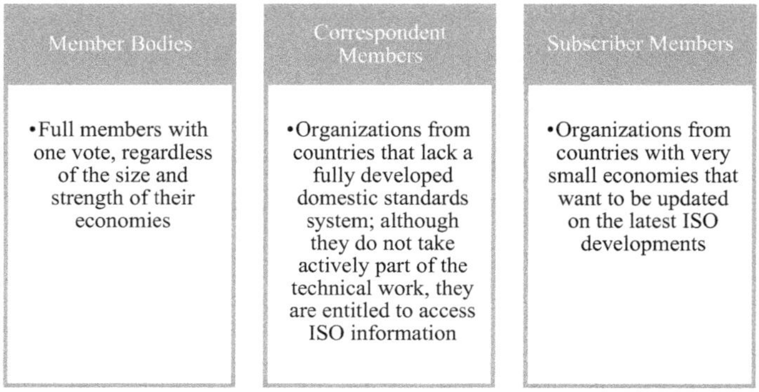

Figure 10: ISO Types of Membership.

Source: Author, based on the ISO Membership Manual

As the figure above indicates, the three member categories enjoy a different level of access and influence over the ISO system. In order to assess the type of membership, fees are calculated in proportion to the country's Gross National Income and trade figures.[178]

ISO Members meet annually at a General Assembly, which deals with proposals from the ISO Council, which in turn meets twice a year. The membership of the ISO Council is based on a yearly rotation to ensure an even representation of all the ISO members. Operative matters related to the day-to-day functioning of the organisation are dealt with by a permanent Secretary General reporting to the ISO President, whose term lasts two years.

3.3.2 The Development and Adoption of ISO Standards

The ISO develops new standards according to their proposal by its Members during the General Assembly.[179] Once the proposal is adopted,

178 ISO Membership Manual, p. 13; ISO, Structure and Governance, available at: <http://www.iso.org/iso/home/about/about_governance.htm> (last visited: 30 June 2015).

179 The ISO standard-setting process available on the Internet addresses only six, instead of eight steps; available at: <http://www.iso.org/iso/home/standards_development/resources-for-technicalwork/stages_of_the_development_of_international_standards.htm> (last visited: 30 June 2015).

the relevant Technical Committee, composed of experts from industrial, business and technical sectors, put forward by ISO members develops the required standard. The ISO has over 250 technical committees, all of them responding to three additional General Policy Development Committees.[180] The subsequent procedure is as follows.

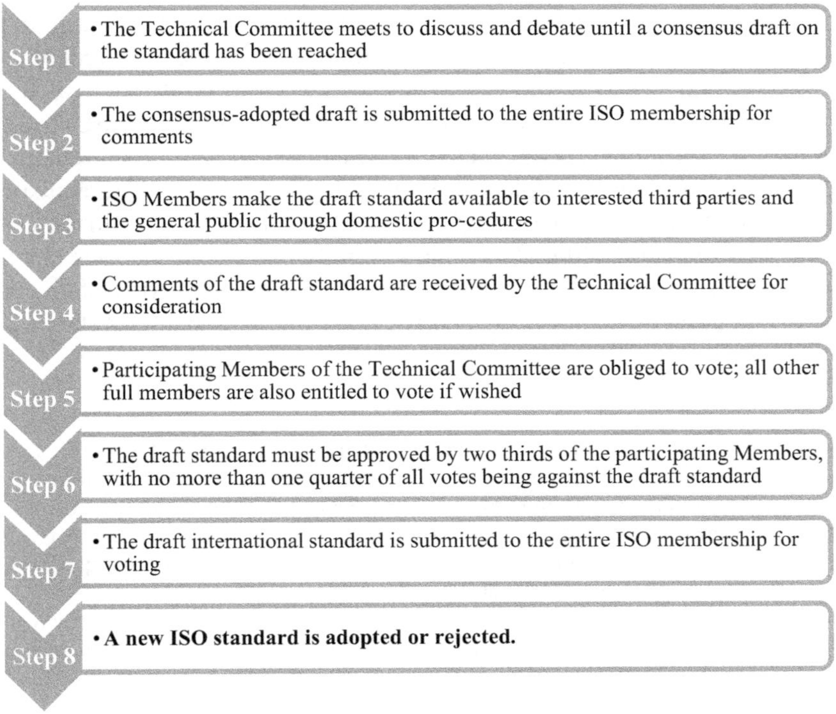

Figure 11: ISO Standard-Setting Procedure.

Source: ISO Website, revised by the Author

ISO standards are entirely voluntary in nature. Due to high quotas of implementation in national legal systems, however, they are invested with a *de facto* mandatory nature that heightens their relevance for market

180 ISO, Who Develops ISO Standards?, available at: <http://www.iso.org/iso/home/standards_development/who-develops-iso-standards.htm> (last visited: 30 June 2015).

access. The recently developed ISO 22000 standards on Food Safety Management are particularly important for trade in foodstuffs.[181] These standards lay down the necessary requirements for the correct implementation of all food safety management systems along the supply chain in order to demonstrate an organisations's ability to control food safety hazards.[182] This standard is complemented by three ISO Technical Specifications: the ISO Technical Specification 22004, which aims at giving implementation guidance to the ISO 22000:2005;[183] the ISO Technical Specification 22003:2013, which defines the rules applicable for the audit and certification of a food management system;[184] and ISO Technical Specifications 22002–1/4:2013, which specifies the requirements for the establishment, implementation and maintenance of prerequisite programs to assist in controlling food safety hazards.[185] As a final mention, ISO Standard 22005:2007 on traceability in the feed and food chain establishes the general principles and basic requirements for system design and implementation.[186] This is the latest international food standard

181 ISO 22000, Food Safety Management Systems – Requirements for Any Organization on the Food Chain; available at: <http://www.iso.org/iso/home/store/catalogue_tc/catalogue_detail.htm?csnumber=35466> (last visited: 30 June 2015).

182 They include feed producers, primary producers, food manufacturers, transport and storage operators, retail and food service establishments, producers of equipment, packaging material, additives and ingredients.

183 ISO Technical Specification ISO/TS 22004:2005; Food Safety Management Systems: Guidance on the Application of ISO 22000:2005; available at: <http://www.iso.org/iso/home/store/catalogue_tc/catalogue_detail.htm?csnumber=39835> (last visited: 30 June 2015).

184 ISO Technical Specification ISO/TS 22003:2013, Food Safety Management Systems: Requirements for Bodies providing Audit and Certification of Food Safety Management Systems; available at: <http://www.iso.org/iso/home/store/catalogue_tc/catalogue_detail.htm?csnumber=39835> (last visited: 30 June 2015).

185 ISO Technical Specification ISO/TS 22002–1/4:2009, Prerequisites Programs for Food Safety: Catering, Food Manufacturing, Farming and Food Packaging Manufacturing; available at: <http://www.iso.org/iso/home/store/catalogue_tc/catalogue_detail.htm?csnumber=44001> (last visited: 30 June 2015).

186 ISO Technical Specification ISO 22005: 2007, Traceability in the Feed and Food Chain: General Principles and Basic Requirements for System Design and Implementation; available at: <http://www.iso.org/iso/home/store/catalogue_tc/catalogue_detail.htm?csnumber=36297> (last visited: 30 June 2015).

adopted by the ISO General Principles and Guidance for System Design and Development.

Similar to the CAC, the number of international food standards adopted by the ISO has increased dramatically to over 1000 to date.[187] This growth has led to an elevated status, which is justified by the direct recognition of the ISO as a relevant international standard-setting organisation in the TBT Agreement. Indeed, according to Article 4.1 of the TBT Agreement, WTO Members must ensure that their national standard bodies comply with the Code of Good Practice, which is in turn an ISO product.[188] The resulting reinforcement of legitimacy is also tangible with the recent amendment of the ISO Statutes, establishing that only national standards bodies can become members. Whereas international standards are only effective after being implemented on their respective domestic levels, the impact of national standards bodies in ensuring harmonisation is evident. Therefore, the next section will analyse the legal nature and judicial implications of the German standard-setting organisation for food, the German Food Code Commission (Food Code Commission).[189]

3.4 Case Study: The German Food Code Commission

The Food Code Commission was established by German Food Law (LFBG) in 2005.[190] Its Code is a collection of guiding principles that describes the necessary requirements that foodstuffs need to meet in order to be placed on the market.[191] These guidelines complement, but do

187 ISO, ISO Standards and Food: Quality and Safety from Farm to Fork, January 2012, p. 3; available at: <http://www.iso.org/iso/iso_and_food.pdf> (last visited: 30 June 2015).

188 Annex 3 of the TBT Agreement: Code of Good Practice for the Preparation, Adoption and Application of Standards [WTO Code of Practice]; see *infra*, Chapter 4, Section III.

189 German Food Code Commission [Food Code Commission] as established in para. 15 of the German Food Law, 1 September 2005, *ger.* Lebensmittel-und Futtermittel-Gesetzbuch, BGBl. I S. 1426 [LFGB].

190 Para. 15.1 of the LBFG.

191 Para. 15.1 of the LFBG.

not substitute, binding law. Yet they are subject to judicial review due to their nature as objective expert opinion. The guidelines express the prevailing public understanding of all those involved in the marketability of foodstuffs. In other words, these guidelines include well-researched production and trade customs in the light of the average consumer's expectations.[192]

Management tasks within the German Food Commission are divided among three main players: the Food Code Commission, the Steering Committee and the Food Code Technical Committees. Their respective duties are complemented by a Secretariat. The German Food Commission develops these guidelines in accordance with international standards.[193] It was established and appointed by the Federal Ministry of Agriculture and Nutrition (BMEL) in agreement with the Federal Ministry of Economics and Technology. It is composed of 32 representatives from academia, official controls, consumers and the private sector equally. Additionally, the BMEL appoints the chairman and his deputy and also issues its rules of procedure.[194]

The Food Code Commission is an independent body. However, it works according to the rules of procedure[195] issued by the BMEL, which endorses the work of the commission by providing a Secretariat and taking on additional costs incurred by the Commission. The BMEL is not a member of the Commission and therefore it does not have the right to vote. The elected members are appointed for a period of five years and belong to one of the represented sectors.[196] Members of the Food Code Commission that cease to belong to the circle which they initially represented can be relieved of office if the BMEL considers it

192 Para. 16.2 of the LFBG.

193 Para. 15.2 of the LFBG.

194 Para. 15.3 of the LFBG.

195 Rules of Procedure of the German Food Code Commission, *ger.* Geschäftsordnung der Deutschen Lebensmittelbuch-Kommission, 25 May 2009, available at: <https://www.bmel.de/SharedDocs/Downloads/Ernaehrung/Lebensmittelbuch/GeschaeftsordnungLebensmittelbuchkommission.pdf;jsessionid=2BD74F-B6EEFB370C315A83D89D9F 2879.2_cid358?__blob=publicationFile> (last visited: 30 June 2015) [Rules of Procedure].

196 Art. 1.1 of the Rules of Procedure.

convenient to do so.[197] While performing their tasks, Members have a duty of confidentiality, which can only be lifted by the BMEL.[198]

3.4.1 The Adoption and Modification of Food Standards

The Food Code Commission makes its impact known by the consensus reached between the parties involved in the decision-making process. The process starts with an invitation to a meeting of the German Food Code Commission, the Steering Committee or a Technical Committee extended by the Secretariat in agreement with their respective chairmen. An invitation is only issued when the majority of the members requests one. The Ministry, however, may convoke a meeting at any time.[199] These meetings are not open to the public.[200] The corresponding Committee decides together with the Ministry whether and to what extent the public will be informed about the course and result of the meetings. The protection of personal information as well as professional and business secrets is therefore guaranteed.[201] Experts may be summoned to attend the meetings of a Technical Committee to advise on the issue under discussion.[202] Should this be the case, no decision will be taken on an advisory opinion in the presence of an expert.[203] The circles represented in the Food Code Commission may request the preparation or modification of guiding principles through a written proposal to its secretariat. The Steering Committee accepts or declines a proposal to prepare or modify a food standard. The standard-setting procedure continues as follows.

197 Art. 1.2 of the Rules of Procedure.
198 Art. 1.3 of the Rules of Procedure.
199 Art. 5.1 of the Rules of Procedure.
200 Art. 5.2 of the Rules of Procedure.
201 Art. 5.4 of the Rules of Procedure.
202 Art. 6.1 of the Rules of Procedure.
203 Art. 6.2 of the Rules of Procedure.

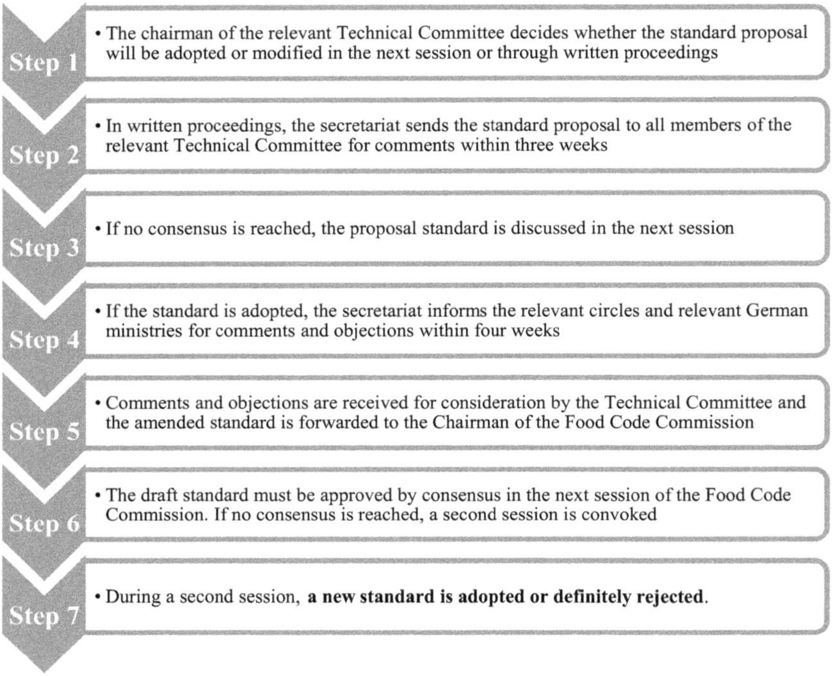

Figure 12: The Standard-Setting Procedure in the German Food Code Commission.

Source: German Food Code Commission, Rules of Procedure, 25 May 2009; revised by the Author.

As the figure above shows, the standard-setting procedure resembles that of other international standard-setting bodies here discussed. The main difference, however, is found in the involvement of the German government in both designing and adopting new food standards. Due to this particular feature, it may be argued that authority and legitimacy levels are higher than in those standard-setting bodies with no governmental intervention.

3.4.2 The Impact of Adopted Food Standards

Adopted food standards are published by the relevant German ministry upon review of their compatibility with domestic legislation. In cases where its publication is not possible due to legal or technical concerns, an adopted standard is remitted back to the chairman of the Food Code Commission for reassessment. This *post facto* legal review is complemented by the ability of the Food Code Commission to make recommendations to the relevant legislative drafters for the modification of domestic legal provisions.[204]

The influence of the German food standards on the domestic courts is tangible. An overview of three selected cases illustrates their acquired position in science-based German judicial review.

3.4.2.1 Ham Case I

In 2010, the German Administrative Court of Aachen (Ham Case I) based its findings on one of the German food standards when it held that the labelling of one product as a pork product was misleading to consumers in cases where the protein content differed from that established by the Food Code Commission.

The court further referred to the relevance of the Food Code Commission in representing the general standard of consumer expectation through its adopted food standards.[205] Hence, a product that is marketed and labelled as 'ham', and which does not comply with the requirements set out for that particular product in the Food Code will be in breach of German Food Law.[206]

3.4.2.2 Ham Case II

The decision was appealed before the Administrative Court of Appeals in Münster (Ham Case II),[207] which upheld the judgment of the court of the first instance. The decision stated that the product in question failed to fulfill the requirements set out in the German Food Code, as well

204 Art. 13 of the Rules of Procedure.

205 The German Administrative Court of Aachen, *ger.* Verwaltungsgericht Aachen, Decision of 30 July 2010, 7 K 1467/09 [VG Aachen].

206 In Germany, protection from misleading information is guaranteed for consumers under Art. 11 of the LBFG.

207 The German Administrative Court of Appeal, North-Rheine Westphalia, *ger.* Oberverwaltungsgericht Nordrhein-Westfalen (OVG NWF), Decision of 16 November 2010, 13A 2108/10 [OVG NWF, Decision of 16 November 2010].

as those stipulated for the same product in the Codex Alimentarius.[208] It further referred to extensive domestic jurisprudence dating back to 1987,[209] whereby the standards adopted by the German Food Code Commission are deemed legitimate tools to assess the legality of foodstuffs marketed in Germany due to the high quality expert opinions involved in the standard-setting process.

3.4.2.3 The Protocol Case

The transparency of the standard-setting process within the German Food Code Commission was at stake in one case before the Administrative Court of Appeals in Münster.[210] In this case, the applicant requested access to the minutes of the meetings held at the Food Code Commission. The request was based on the German Freedom of Information Act (IFG).[211] The court held that the applicant had no right to access the requested documents of the Food Code Commission due to two main reasons. First, the court stated that although the Food Code Commission was embedded in public law, and as such the IFG would apply to its activities, it is not completely integrated with the relevant ministry. Second, in cases where the necessary confidentiality of the documents is compromised, an exception clause in the IFG may be called upon. The court considered the minutes of the Food Code Commission as confidential briefings within the meaning of the IFG exception clause because their release to the public would substantially hinder independent and impartial deliberations within the Food Code Committees.[212]

208 OVG NWF, Decision of 16 November 2010, para. 7.

209 The German Federal Administrative Court, *ger.* Bundesverwaltungsgericht (BVerwG), Decision of 10 December 1987, 3 C 18.87, with further references.

210 The German Administrative Court of Appeal, North-Rheine Westphalia, OVG NWF, Decision of 2 November 2010, 8A 475/10 [OVG NRW, Decision of 2 November 2010].

211 German Freedom of Information Act, *ger.* Gesetz zur Regelung des Zugangs zu Informationen des Bundes (Informationsfreiheitsgesetz – IFG), 5 September 2005, BGBl. I S. 2722.

212 OVG NRW, Decision of 2 November 2010.

3.4.3 Closing Remarks

An analysis of the German Food Code Commission has highlighted both the advantages and shortcomings of domestic food standard-setting. As an institution embedded in public law, the Food Code Commission has proved successful in functioning with acceptable levels of transparency and recognised expert authority. The judicial endorsement of the Food Code, along with the comprehensive representation of the relevant food industry players, adds the legitimacy on which the Food Commission relies. In addition, its decisions are largely based on scientific principles and on existing international food standards. Unlike standard-setting procedures within the CAC[213] and ISO,[214] the German Food Code Commission follows a relatively short decision-making process to adopt new food standards or modify existing ones. Similar to the significance attributed to the relevant international food standards within the WTO system, however, the use of German Food Code standards will imply a presumption of compliance with (domestic) food legislation. Therefore, an increase in the adoption of science-based standards, along with an alignment with the relevant international food standards is essential to guarantee the effective functioning of the German Food Code system.

3.5 Conclusion

The WTO obligation to base domestic measures on relevant international standards, as well as their direct reference in the WTO agreements, has contributed to the increasing importance of standard-setting bodies in food trade. This development reflects the role played by international and national standard-setting bodies in the creation of new forms of food governance. Hence, the third chapter described the legal mechanisms of the two most relevant standard-setting bodies for international trade in food: the CAC and the ISO. In doing this, section II examined

213 See *supra*, Section II.
214 See *supra*, Section III.

the CAC and its rules of procedure, as well as the development and adoption of food standards. Section III turned to the ISO, its rules for membership, the development of standards and its adoption procedures.

The importance given to membership openness in international standard-setting bodies, as defined by the Appellate Body in US Tuna II (Mexico), highlighted the need to assess membership mechanisms. While this aspect is undisputed in so far as the CAC is concerned, the legal status of ISO membership was rather uncertain until recently. After the amendment of its Statutes in 2012, whereby individuals and companies are no longer eligible for ISO membership, the balance between WTO case law and legitimacy principles was able to be restored.

Although the relevant international standards are devised by global experts, it is only after their implementation at the domestic level that food standards become effective. Therefore, the important role played by national standards bodies justified an analysis of their mechanisms and functions at the domestic level. As an illustrative example, the last section examined the legal mechanisms and judicial relevance of the Food Code Commission in Germany and gave a context to the challenges posed by consensus-driven standard-setting bodies.

The next chapter will examine the legal implications of food standards as technical barriers to trade. It will therefore be devoted to a legal analysis of the relevant provisions in the TBT Agreement.

4. Food Quality Standards as Technical Barriers to Trade

4.1 What is Food Quality and Why does it Matter?

The controversy over the existence of an accurate definition for food quality has unsurprisingly been subject to lively debate.[215] In particular, the concept of food quality remains vague in all cases where legislation pursues a dual objective, that of regulating market access requirements, while eliminating trade barriers.[216]

One line of thought argues that food legislation on compositional standards cannot exist without a tangible food quality concept.[217] Following the same line, the WHO defined food quality as a series of attributes that influence the value of a product for the consumer. It further identified negative and positive attributes of food quality. Negative attributes include spoilage, contamination with dirt, discolouration and off-odours; whereas, positive attributes are those such as origin, colour, flavour, texture and processing methods.[218] This traditional theory considers food

215 See *inter alia*: Anna Giusti/Enrico Bignetti/Carlo Canella, 'Exploring New Frontiers in Total Food Quality Definition and Assessment: from Chemical to Neurochemical Properties' (2008) 1 (2) Food and Bioprocess Technology, pp. 130–142; Claudio Peri, 'The Universe of Food Quality' (2006) 1–2 Food Quality and Preferences, pp. 3–8.

216 *Cf.* Erin Holleran/Maury Bredahl/Lokman Zaibet, 'Private Incentives for Adopting Food Safety and Quality Assurance' (2004) 24 (6) Food Policy, pp. 669–683; Dawn Thilmany/Christopher Barrett, 'Regulatory Barriers in an Integrated World Food Market' (1997) 19 (2) Appl. Econ. Perspect. Pol., pp. 91–107.

217 Raymond O'Rourke, European Food Law, 3rd ed., Sweet and Maxwell 2005, p. 101 [O'Rourke]; Alemanno, pp. 51–60.

218 Joint FAO/WHO Food Standards Program, 'Assuring Food Safety and Quality: Guidelines for Strengthening National Food Control Systems' FAO Food and Nutrition Paper Nr. 76, Rome 2003, p. 2; available at: <http://www.who.int/foodsafety/publications> (last visited: 30 June 2015) [FAO/WHO, Food Safety and Quality].

safety as a *conditio sine qua non* for quality, according to which a product is of quality if it can demonstrate the absence of fraud, defect and adulteration.[219] It follows that food safety qualifies as a static element in consumers' expectations, while food quality enjoys a more dynamic characteristic that changes according to time and circumstances. The frequent confusion between the concepts of food safety and quality poses a legal challenge in determining the scope of application of domestic (and international) food laws.[220]

Likewise, the ISO developed a widely-used definition of quality as the totality of features and characteristics of a product that bear on its ability to satisfy stated or implied needs. Hence, as food quality essentially depends on objective product characteristics and individual subjective preferences, its concept is inherently difficult to define.[221] This is because the concept of quality has been reshaped as a response mechanism for newer and higher consumer demands, and as such it has evolved today into an autonomous concept that is somewhat detached from safety aspects, gravitating towards the idea of free trade flow.

Whereas food quality qualifies as a characteristic of an identifiable product, the rules governing technical requirements in international trade will apply. Technical requirements ensure not only safe products, but also interoperability among different components of a given good to guarantee market access. Therefore, harmonisation of technical standards, although very difficult to achieve, has proved essential to ensure free trade. Because WTO Law provides substantive and procedural rules to distinguish artificial requirements that disguise protectionism,[222] an assessment of the TBT Agreement as an adequate legal framework to overcome differences among global technical standards[223] justifies the following analysis.

219 FAO/WHO, Food Safety and Quality, p. 2.

220 FAO/WHO, Food Safety and Quality, p. 3.

221 Smith, para. 18.

222 Thomas Cottier/Matthias Oesch, International Trade Regulation: Law and Policy in the WTO, the European Union and Switzerland: Cases, Materials and Comments, Stämpfli 2005, p. 750 *et seq*.

223 Robert Howse, 'A New Device for Creating International Legal Normativity: The WTO Technical Barriers to Trade Agreement and 'International Standards'' in: Christian Joerges/Ernst-Ulrich Petersmann (eds), Constitutionalism, Multilevel Trade Governance and Social Regulation, Hart Publishing 2006, pp. 383–395.

Therefore, this chapter is divided as follows. Section II provides a historical overview of the TBT Agreement to put the legal implications of (food) standards into context. Section III addresses the concept of technical regulation under the TBT Agreement. In doing so, it follows the three-tier test developed in WTO Case Law. The analysis on substantive rules relevant for standardisation continues in section IV with the examination of the definition of standards under the TBT Agreement. Before concluding, section V addresses the concept of non-governmental bodies and their relevance for food standard-setting bodies.

4.2 From Tokyo to Uruguay: A Summary of the Historical Development of the TBT Agreement

The TBT Agreement originated during the 1973–1979 Tokyo Round multilateral trade negotiations, which culminated in the adoption of the Standards Code Agreement (SCA).[224] The Code provided a voluntary framework for reducing or removing technical barriers to trade by addressing the preparation, adoption and application of technical regulations and standards.

Decades later, the substantive provisions of the SCA and its unresolved issues, such as reciprocal testing, certification arrangements and access to certification systems, were a focal topic for negotiations during the Uruguay Round.[225] It was at that time that two groups were formed: those dealing with measures relating to technical barriers to trade and

224 Agreement on Technical Barriers to Trade, 12 April 1979, 1186 UNTS 276, GATT, BISD, 26th Supp 8 (1980) [Tokyo Standards Code Agreement]. For an overview of the Tokyo Round Negotiations *see*: ALAN SYKES, Product Standards for Internationally Integrated Good Markets, Brookings Institution 1995, pp. 70–77 [SYKES, Product Standards 1995]. For a detailed history of the SCA *see*: TERENCE STEWART (ed.), The GATT Uruguay Round: A Negotiating History, Kluwer Law & Taxation 1993, pp. 1067 *et seq.*

225 JEFFREY BELSON, Certification Marks, Sweet & Maxwell 2002, p. 95.

those dealing with animal, plant material and human health.[226] The TBT Agreement thus retained the original obligations imposed by the SCA while refining the framework for economic regulation.[227] It has done so through derived rules backed up by institutional mechanism.[228] As a result of the comprehensive inclusion and successful adoption of the TBT Agreement, the Tokyo Round TBT Committee decided to terminate the SCA in 1995.[229]

4.3 The Concept of Technical Regulation

The TBT Agreement addresses the preparation, adoption and application of technical regulations in its Articles 2 and 3.[230] It draws a distinction between those measures adopted by central government bodies[231] and those adopted by local governmental and non-governmental bodies.[232] In order to assess whether these provisions find application, it is important to determine what constitutes a technical regulation. Annex 1.1 of the TBT Agreement establishes that a technical regulation is:

226 These negotiations resulted later in the adoption of the SPS Agreement. See also: ALEMANNO, p. 239 *et seq.*

227 Analysing the legal implications of the Tokyo Round for the TBT Agreement see: SIMON LESTER/WILLIAM STEMBERG, 'The GATT Origins of TBT Agreement Article 2.1 and 2.2' (2014) 17 (1) Journal of International Economic Law, pp. 215–232.

228 PATRICK MACRORY/ARTHUR APPLETON/MICHAEL PLUMMER (eds), The World Trade Organization: Legal, Economic and Political Analysis, Vol. I, Springer 2005, pp. 375–376; SHERRY STEPHENSON, 'Standards and Conformity Assessment as Nontariff Barriers to Trade' Policy Research Working Paper Nr. 1826, The World Bank Development Research Group, September 1997, pp. 38–40.

229 GATT, Tokyo Round Committee on TBT, Termination of the Tokyo Round Agreement on Technical Barriers to Trade, 20 October 1995, TBT/40 Special Distribution.

230 LUDIVINE TAMIOTTI, 'Article 2 and 3 TBT' in: RÜDIGER WOLFRUM/PETER-TOBIAS STOLL/ANJA SEIBERT-FOHR (eds), WTO – Technical Barriers and SPS Measures, Vol. III, Martinus Hijhoff Publishers 2007, pp. 210–242.

231 Art. 2 of the TBT Agreement.

232 Art. 3 of the TBT Agreement.

> [a] document which lays down product characteristics or their related processes and production methods, including the applicable administrative provisions, with which compliance is mandatory. It may also include or deal exclusively with terminology, symbols, packaging, marking or labelling requirements as they apply to a product, process or production method.

This definition has been clarified by the Appellate Body in *EC – Abestos*[233] and in *EC – Sardines*,[234] whereby three requirements must be fulfilled for a measure to be considered a technical regulation: the product to which the measure applies must be identifiable; the measure must lay down certain characteristics for that product; and the measure must be mandatory.[235] This precedent was confirmed in US – Tuna II, where the Appellate Body stated that the nature of a measure must be determined according to the characteristics of that measure on a case-by-case basis.[236]

4.3.1 Identifiable Product

The first tier of the technical regulation test refers to the identifiability of a product to which the technical regulation applies. The product must be identifiable, but not necessarily named, identified or specified in the regulation. In the words of the Appellate Body:

> [...] [T]here may be perfectly sound administrative reasons for formulating a "technical regulation" in a way that does not expressly identify products by name, but simply makes them identifiable – for instance, through the 'characteristic' that is the subject of regulation.[237]

Therefore, compliance with the first tier requires the identification of product coverage provided in a given technical requirement.

233 WTO Appellate Body Report, *European Communities – Measures Affecting Asbestos and Asbestos-Containing Products*, 12 March 2001, WTO/AB/DS135 [*EC-Asbestos*] para. 66–70.

234 *EC – Sardines*, para. 176.

235 *EC – Asbestos*, paras. 60–70.

236 *US – Tuna II (Mexico)*, para. 188.

237 *EC – Asbestos*, para. 70.

4.3.2 Characteristics of the Product

The second tier of the technical regulation test requires it to lay down certain characteristics of the identifiable product. Product characterisation must be interpreted in accordance with its ordinary meaning, that is, any objectively definable feature, quality, attribute or other distinguishing mark of a product. It may also refer to a product's composition, size, shape, colour, texture, hardness, tensile strength, flammability, conductivity, density or viscosity.[238]

4.3.3 Mandatory Measure

The third tier of the technical regulation test is self-evident in that it refers to the wording of the definition given in Annex 1.1 of the TBT Agreement. A measure is deemed to be mandatory if it regulates the characteristics of an identifiable product in a binding or compulsory fashion[239] and if it is directly applicable to all WTO Members.[240]

4.4 Standards under the TBT Agreement

The TBT Agreement addresses the preparation, adoption and application of standards in its Article 4. Annex 1.2 defines standards as:

> Document approved by a recognized body, that provides, for common and repeated use, rules, guidelines or characteristics for products or related processes and production methods, with which compliance is not mandatory. It may also include or deal exclusively with terminology, symbols, packaging, marking or labelling requirements as they apply to a product, process or production method.

It is important to note here the distinction drawn by the Appellate Body between the concept of 'standard' as applied to the provisions of the

238 *EC – Asbestos*, para. 67; *EC – Sardines*, para. 189.
239 *EC – Asbestos*, para. 68.
240 *EC – Sardines*, para. 194.

TBT Agreement (such as Article 4) and the term 'international standard' as defined in the ISO/IEC Guide 2. The former will apply in case of disparity with the latter.[241]

In turn, Article 4.1 of the TBT Agreement embodies a compromise between the limited authority of central governments to compel local and non-governmental bodies and the maintenance of rights and obligations arising out of the TBT Agreement. It reads:

> Members shall ensure that their central government standardizing bodies accept and comply with the Code of Good Practice for the Preparation, Adoption and Application of Standards in Annex 3 to this Agreement [...] They shall take such reasonable measures as may be available to them to ensure that local government and non-governmental standardizing bodies within their territories, as well as regional standardizing bodies of which they or one or more bodies within their territories are members, accept and comply with this Code of Good Practice. [...].[242]

The WTO Code of Good Practice plays a fundamental role in ensuring compliance with the obligations set out in the TBT Agreement. It vests the ISO with a newly found legitimacy as the relevant standard-setting body within the TBT legal framework. In turn, the ISO has amended its membership rules so as to no longer allow individuals and private companies to become members, but to limit access to national standard bodies or, in the language of Article 4.1 of the TBT Agreement, central government standardising bodies only. Furthermore, acceptance and compliance with the WTO Code of Good Practice by central, local and non-governmental bodies creates a presumption of compliance with the TBT Agreement:

> Standardizing bodies that have accepted and are complying with the Code of Good Practice shall be acknowledged by the Members as complying with the principles of this Agreement.[243]

By indirectly but explicitly recognising the legal status of the ISO, Article 4.2 of the TBT Agreement extends its scope of application to virtually all the players involved in trade. This is all the more so in cases where the legal nature of the standard-setting body is disputed. Thus, a compliance

241 *EC – Sardines*, para. 224.

242 Art. 4.1 of the TBT Agreement.

243 Art. 4.2 of the TBT Agreement.

test must be carried out in order to determine the applicability of WTO law for measures affecting trade in food.

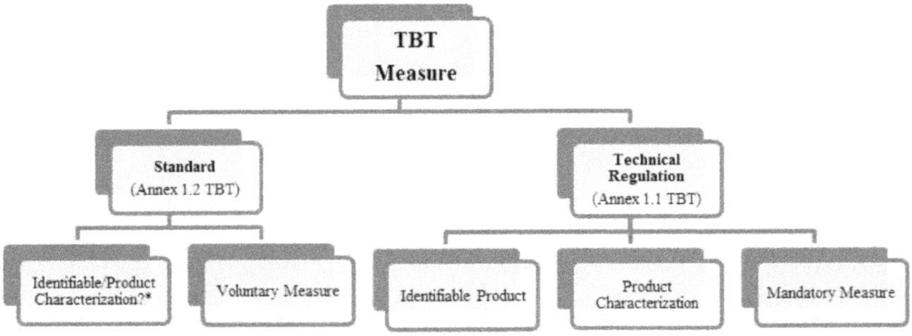

Figure 13: TBT Applicability Test.

Source: Author

* No jurisprudence to date; in analogy to *EC – Asbestos* and *EC – Sardines*

As the figure above illustrates, the nature of the measure must be first determined in accordance with the definitions give in Annex 1.1 and 1.2 of the TBT Agreement. Once this has been assessed, the corresponding provisions of the TBT Agreement will apply. Technical regulations will fall under the scope of Articles 2 and 3, while the provision addressing standards is found in Article 4.

Unlike technical regulations, measures falling under the definition of standards will require a further assessment as established in Annex 3 of the TBT Agreement. A presumption of compliance with the TBT Agreement applies in cases where the incumbent standard-setting body has adopted the WTO Code of Good Practice. In other cases, there is a reverse burden of proof to establish TBT compliance.

Article 4 of the TBT Agreement does not impose upon Members the duty to guarantee compliance with the Code of Good Practice.[244] However, it does impose the obligation to respect the principle of non-discrimination[245] and to avoid the creation of unnecessary barriers to trade.[246] Unlike Article 3 of the TBT Agreement, Member States are not obliged to formulate and implement measures and mechanisms for non-central

244 As established in Annex 1 of the TBT Agreement.

245 Annex 3.D of the TBT Agreement.

246 Annex 3.E of the TBT Agreement.

government bodies.[247] However, Member States are proscribed from requiring or encouraging standardisation bodies to act inconsistently with the Code of Good Practice.[248]

4.5 Non-Governmental Bodies under the TBT Agreement

In principle, Members are responsible for all acts and omissions of its organs, including local and non-governmental standardising bodies. However, the TBT Agreement is clear in that it dictates the adoption of 'such reasonable measures as may be available' in order to diminish the burden on Members with a federal, decentralised system. Although there is no clear-cut line, the endorsement of private actions by governments creates a direct line of attribution that allows the application of (public) International Law. For instance, in *Japan – Film*, the WTO Panel stated that:

> [...] the fact that an action is taken by private parties does not rule out the possibility that it may be deemed to be governmental if there is sufficient governmental involvement with it.[249]

In determining what constitutes sufficient governmental involvement, the panel referred to previous GATT cases[250] and added that it is difficult to draw clear-cut lines and thus, the possibility needs to be examined on a case-by-case basis.[251] The definition of a non-governmental body can be found in Annex 1.8 of the TBT Agreement, which reads:

247 As established in Art. 3 in conjunction with Art. 2.2 of the TBT Agreement.

248 Art. 4.2 of the TBT Agreement.

249 WTO Panel Report, *Japan – Measures Affecting Consumer Photographic Film and Paper*, 22 April 1998, WT/DS44/R, para. 10.56 [*Japan – Film*].

250 GATT Panel Report, *European Economic Community – Restrictions on Imports of Dessert Apples* (Complaint by Chile), 18 April 1989, L/6491 – 36S/93; GATT Panel Report, *Japan – Trade in Semi-Conductors*, 4 May 1988, L/6309 – 35S/116.

251 *Japan – Film*, para. 10.56.

Body other than a central government body or a local government body, including a non-governmental body that has legal power to enforce technical regulation.

The negative definition leaves a large margin of appreciation for judicial review, whereby non-governmental bodies may engage in the development of single standards while their main activity focuses on conducting other types of business.[252] However, an historic interpretation of this provision suggests that its scope of application does not encompass those non-governmental bodies that only occasionally set standards. An explanatory note to the definition of the term 'standard' during the Tokyo Round specified that the definition did not cover technical specifications prepared by an individual company for its own production or consumption requirements.[253]

The apparent contradiction between the historical and the quasi-judicial interpretation to the definition of non-governmental bodies has not attracted any further interest within the TBT Committee.[254] Although concerns about the use of so-called private or commercial standards have been raised by some Members, the issue was not pursued further.

4.6 Conclusion

While the importance of international (food) standards appears undisputed to date, the legal architecture to which they are subject is not yet clear. This chapter, by attempting to define food quality, has shown that

252 *US – Tuna II (Mexico)*, para. 360.

253 Committee on Sanitary and Phytosanitary Measures, Private Voluntary Standards Within the WTO Multilateral Framework, Submission by the United Kingdom to the Committee on Sanitary and Phytosanitary Measures, 9 October 2007, WTO/G/SPS/GEN/802, p. 74.

254 Denise Prèvost, 'Private Sector Food Safety Standards and the SPS Agreement: Challenges and Possibilities' (2008) 33 South African Yearbook of International Law, pp. 1–37, p. 28, with reference to: Committee on Sanitary and Phytosanitary Measures, Summary of the Meeting Held on 29–30 June 2005, Note by the Secretariat, 18 August 2005, G/SPS/R37/Rev. 1.

it qualifies as a characteristic of an identifiable product, and thus the rules governing technical requirements in international trade apply.

After a brief overview of the genesis of the TBT Agreement and its predecessor the SCA, section III addressed the legal definition of technical regulation under the TBT Agreement. In doing so, it analysed established WTO Case Law and the three-tier test to determine whether a technical regulation falls within the scope of Articles 2 and 3 of the TBT Agreement. Section IV examined the concept of 'standard' in the light of Annex 1.2 of the TBT Agreement as well as according to case law. It concluded by stating that the elevated level status of the ISO extends the TBT scope of application to virtually all the players involved in an international transaction. This line of argument led to an analysis of the definition given to non-governmental bodies under the TBT Agreement, which due to the lack of jurisprudence in this regard, remains widely unsettled.

Continuing with the legal analysis on the implications of food quality standards in international trade, the next chapter will examine the role of intellectual property rights in general and Trademark Law in particular within the existing legal framework for food (labelling) standards.

5. Food Labelling Standards and Trademark Law

5.1 Consumer Protection and Food Labelling

At the crossroads between the TBT Agreement and the TRIPS Agreement, food labelling measures pose a higher risk of being potentially discriminatory against imported foodstuffs. It is widely-known that WTO Members have increasingly relied on labelling standards to regulate market access by requiring the display of certain information in order to guarantee consumer protection.[255] The ultimate aim of such policies is to allow market players to make more informed choices. The fact that product labelling responds quicker to consumer demands and so contributes to shape consumers' habits[256] may result in alterations to the flow of international food trade. Whereas consumer protection is interpreted as the underlying reason for the adoption of food quality standards, the Appellate Body reports in *US – Tuna II (Mexico)* and *US – COOL* show that they are often used as justification for the imposition of trade-distortionary measures. Likewise, trademark rights are known to confer upon their holders an exclusive and absolute right against third parties and as such, it is disputed whether their use through food labelling standards results in trade-distorting behaviour.

The rationale behind intellectual property protection is undisputed in as far as it grants an incentive to innovate through a legal monopoly

255 Tania Voon/Andrew Mitchell/Catherine Gascoigne, 'Consumer Information, Consumer Preferences and Product Labels under the TBT Agreement' in: Michael Trebilcock/Tracey Epps (eds), Research Handbook on the WTO and Technical Barriers to Trade, Edward Elgar 2013, pp. 454–484 [Voon/Mitchell/Gascoigne].

256 Voon/Mitchell/Gascoigne, p. 454. See *also*: Jill McCluskey/Jason Winfree, 'Pre-Empting Public Regulation with Private Food Quality Standards' (2009) 36 (4) European Review of Agricultural Economics, pp. 525–539.

that benefits society in general.[257] In spite of this common understanding, the response to the increasing legal challenges posed by tensions arising out of the interface of intellectual property rights and market access has been the object of great interest in academic research.[258] Yet the answers to these questions present a major and complex legal picture.[259] While the absence of a food label is considered a disadvantage for market access,[260] the next sections will analyse the legal framework for trademarks in international food trade.

The rationale underlying this chapter is that there is a dichotomy between trademark protection and market access within the WTO legal system, which must be assessed in the light of the current impact of international standards. While section II will examine the origins of the TRIPS Agreement, section III will focus on an analysis of the definition, taxonomy and function of trademarks in international law. After establishing that (food) quality is both a means and aim of trademarks, section IV addresses the legal framework applicable to trademarks in WTO law. In doing so, it will first determine what constitutes a trademark under Article 15.1 of the TRIPS Agreement to later focus on the rights conferred to trademark owners under Article 16.1. The exceptions

257 WIPO, WIPO Intellectual Property Handbook: Policy, Law and Use, 2nd Ed., 2004, para. 1.1 [WIPO Handbook].

258 See *generally*: JOSEF DREXL, Research Handbook on Intellectual Property and Competition Law, Edward Elgar Publishing 2010; STEVEN ANDERMAN, The Interface between Intellectual Property Rights and Competition Law, Cambridge University Press 2007; GUSTAVO GHIDINI, Intellectual Property and Competition Law: The Innovation Nexus, Edward Elgar Publishing 2006.

259 RETO HILTY, 'Individual, Multiple and Collective Ownership: What Impact on Competition?' in: JAN ROSEN (ed), Individualism and Collectiveness in Intellectual Property Law, Edward Elgar Publishing 2012, pp. 3–44, p. 5. [HILTY].

260 Subject to the analysis carried out within the SPS Committee in assessing the impact of food standards on international trade, most participating countries indicated that compliance with (food) standards does not necessarily deliver a price premium despite the investments needed for certification. See: COMMITTEE ON SANITARY AND PHYTOSANITARY MEASURES, Effects of SPS-Related Private Standards: Descriptive Report, 15 June 2009, G/SPS/GEN/932, para. 32. This chapter is partly based on previous published work; see MARIELA MAIDANA-ELETTI, 'Food Labelling and Trademark Law', Max Planck Encyclopedia of Public International Law, Oxford University Press 2014.

to trademark rights under Article 17 and the special trademark requirements in Article 20 of the TRIPS Agreement will also be addressed. Section V briefly concludes.

5.2 A Summary of the Historical Development of the TRIPS Agreement on Trademarks

With the creation of the WTO regime,[261] after the Marrakesh Agreement trade-related policy choices and directions took over the once agnostic approach followed by the GATT. As such, the TRIPS Agreement entails detailed requirements on the content of Members' domestic laws for their coverage of the protection of intellectual property rights and their enforcement mechanisms.

Notwithstanding the successful attempt at achieving a certain degree of harmonisation, there is ample room for legal disputes to arise. By granting exclusive rights, intellectual property law limits market access, and thus, competition. However, it has been argued that a lack of intellectual property protection leads to a distortion of competition to the extent that it reduces the necessary incentives to liberalise market access.[262] As a reflection of this, the negotiations during the Uruguay Round leading to the inclusion of TRIPS in the WTO Agreements were of a most controversial nature.[263] Initially, developing countries showed opposition.[264]

261 LAURENCE HELFER, 'Regime Shifting: The TRIPS Agreement and New Dynamics of International Intellectual Property Lawmaking' (2004) 29 (1) Yale Journal of International Law, pp. 1–83, p. 10.

262 THOMAS COTTIER/INGO MEITINGER, 'The TRIPS Agreement without a Competition Agreement?' Fondazione Eni Enrico Mettei, Trade and Competition in the WTO and Beyond, Venice 1998, p. 3.

263 For a detailed discussion *see*: SUSAN SELL, Power and Ideas: North-South Politics of Intellectual Property and Antitrust, State University of New York Press 1998, p. 132.

264 See *e.g.* the position of India with regard to trademarks, GATT, *Standards and Principles concerning the Availability, Scope and Use of Trade-Related Aspects of Intellectual Property Rights*, 10 July 1989, MTN.GNG/NG11/W/37; and the position of Brazil with regard to enforcement issues, GATT, *Submission by Brazil*, 31 October 1988, MTG.GNG/NG11/W/30.

However, due to their lack of negotiation leverage, and after taking into consideration the threat of exclusion from market access granted by the Generalized System of Preferences,[265] the developing countries eventually gave in to its allure and agreed on an institutionalised framework for intellectual property protection that would provide a dispute settlement mechanism to be included in the negotiations. Indeed, the adoption of TRIPS was largely motivated by the desire to avoid trade-distorting behaviour resulting from widely differing standards in the protection and enforcement of intellectual property rights, as well as by the lack of a harmonised multilateral legal framework dealing with them.[266]

The TRIPS Agreement succeeded in enhancing pre-existing international intellectual property law[267] and in introducing harmonised rules of protection into the multilateral trading system for the first time that include, but are not limited to, the application of basic principles of International Trade Law and intellectual property agreements, a minimum standard of protection of intellectual property rights, their enforcement and dispute settlement mechanisms, and special transitional arrangements to guarantee compliance with the new system.

265 GATT, *Generalized System of Preferences*, Decision of 25 June 1971, BISD 18S/24, p. 24, in which the GATT Contracting Parties agreed on waiving the provisions of Article I for a period of ten years to the extent necessary to permit developed contracting parties to accord preferential treatment to products originating in developing countries without according such treatment to like products of other contracting parties. See *also*: GATT, *Differential and More Favourable Treatment, Reciprocity and Fuller Participation of Developing Countries*, Decision of 28 November 1979, L/4903, p. 1, allowing GATT developed countries to apply preferential treatment to products originating in developing countries in accordance with the GPS, without according such treatment to other contracting parties.

266 Richard Steinberg, 'Trade-Environment Negotiations in the EU, NAFTA and WTO: Regional Trajectories of Rule Development' (1997) 91 American Journal of International Law 1997, pp. 231–232.

267 In particular, the Paris Convention.

5.3 Trademarks and their Role in Food Trade

The relevance of intellectual property law for international trade in food can be drawn from both the predominately economic nature and essentiality of trademarks. At the crossroads between food safety and quality, the need to label a product, whether it is by means of a trademarked brand or a sign of origin, remains essential for successful market access. Accordingly, it is necessary to establish the definition, taxonomy and function of trademarks.

5.3.1 Definition of Trademarks

Marks are defined as signs used to distinguish goods and services during the course of trade.[268] In principle, marks offer businesses the opportunity to establish an exclusive link with a distinctive sign.[269] They serve many functions, among which the guarantee of origin, quality, communication and advertising are of a protected nature.[270] As such, in cases where a recognised mark is used, consumers will assume that a given product is safer or of higher quality.[271] According to public perception, a mark represents the connection between the trademark owner and the goods for which that trademark is used.[272] Moreover, a mark communicates to the consumer a certain image, thus creating an attraction towards the good bearing it.[273] However, not all marks are subject to the same set of rules. Different categories determine the application of different legal provisions and afforded protection.[274] A classification of trademarks is therefore necessary.

268 Tobias Cohen Jehoram/Constant van Nispen/Tony Huydecoper, European Trademark Law: Community Trademark Law and Harmonized National Trademark Law, Wolters Kluwer 2010, p. 5 [Cohen Jehoram *et al.*].
269 Cohen Jehoram *et al.*, p. 6.
270 Karl-Heinz Fezer, Markenrecht, 4th ed., C.H. Beck 2009, paras. 1–20.
271 United Nations Industrial Development Organization (UNIDO), 'Product Quality: A Guide for Small and Medium-Sized Enterprises' Working Paper, Vienna 2006, p. 23.
272 Cohen Jehoram *et al.*, p. 6.
273 Cohen Jehoram *et al.*, p. 6.
274 Cohen Jehoram *et al.*, p. 6.

5.3.2 *The Taxonomy of Trademarks*

There are two main categories of trademark: individual and collective marks. The latter can be divided into three subcategories: conventional collective marks, geographical indication marks and guarantee or certification marks.

5.3.2.1 *Individual Marks*

Individual marks are those used by an individual manufacturer to distinguish his products from those of a competitor.[275] In order to enable consumers to individualise products, the mark must also indicate its source.[276] Thus, individual marks always originate from the same existing business.[277]

5.3.2.2 *Collective Marks*

Collective marks are used collectively by several manufacturers in a group to indicate either common origin or common qualities of their goods.[278] They are used by the trademark owner, his licensees, as well as companies marketing a given good.[279] They may even facilitate the diffusion of relevant market information about certain characteristics of a given product using that trademark.[280] This in turn benefits consumers and ultimately has a positive impact on competition.[281] There are three types of collective mark: conventional collective marks, geographical indication marks and certification marks.

275 Cohen Jehoram *et al.*, p. 6.

276 WIPO Handbook, para. 2.319.

277 Cohen Jehoram *et al.*, p. 124.

278 Cohen Jehoram *et al.*, p. 124; Alexander Peukert, 'The Competitive Significance of Collective Trademarks' in: Jan Rosen (ed): Individualism and Collectiveness in Intellectual Property Law, Edward Elgar Publishing 2012, pp. 241–254 [Peukert].

279 Peukert, p. 241.

280 Hilty, p. 20.

281 Hilty, p. 20; Shahid Alikhan/Raghunath Mashelkar, Intellectual Property and Competitive Strategies in the 21st Century, 2nd ed., Kluwer Law International 2009, p. 14 [Alikhan/Mashelkar].

Conventional collective marks distinguish those goods produced by members of one association from those goods produced by other groups.[282] They are held by associations that are established by means of a private agreement that governs all matters related to the use of the collective mark.[283] Unlike individual marks, the refusal of protection based on public interest[284] applies to both the collective mark and the internal agreement of the association holding the exclusive right.[285]

Another subcategory of collective marks consists of designations indicating the geographical origin of goods during the course of trade.[286] However, the right holder cannot prevent a third party from using that same indication of origin if it is in accordance with honest commercial practices.[287] Thus, the aim of these marks is to designate the origin of goods as being produced by members of a specific association, thus conveying to consumers the information that the business using that sign belongs to an association from that particular geographical area.[288]

Lastly, certification marks are owned by an association of goods.[289] They distinguish goods produced by members of one association from those goods of other groups in accordance with their origin, nature, quality, accuracy, materials used, mode of manufacture, regional origin, source of labour and morality.[290] They also distinguish goods in accordance with certain features originating from different companies under the control

282 PEUKERT, p. 241.

283 PEUKERT, p. 241.

284 Art. 7 bis (2) of the Paris Convention: 'Each country shall be the judge of the particular conditions under which a collective mark shall be protected and may refuse protection if the mark is contrary to the public interest.' This provision has been incorporated into TRIPS by virtue of its Art. 2.1.

285 For a short analysis of EU competition law to horizontal cooperation agreements *see*: PEUKERT, p. 242.

286 COHEN JEHORAM *et al.*, p. 454.

287 COHEN JEHORAM *et al.*, p. 454.

288 PEUKERT, p. 243.

289 PEUKERT, p. 243.

290 RICHARD STIM, Patent, Copyright & Trademark: An Intellectual Property Desk Reference, 12th ed., Bang Printing 2012, p. 400; RICHARD MANN/BARRY ROBERTS, Smith and Roberson's Business Law, 14th ed., South-Western Cengage Learning 2009, p. 845.

of the right holder and are determined by its intended use as well.[291] Furthermore, certification marks convey additional information, and are invested with a broader protection than conventional collective marks. As a result, the competitive advantage of using certification marks has already been recognised in different jurisdictions. Finally, a certification mark is assigned after compliance with a set of certain defined standards has been established. Unlike collective marks, their use is not confined to any membership.[292] They may even be used in combination with individual trademarks.

5.3.3 The Functions of Trademarks

Although in traditional trademark theory origin and quality have been recognised as the two main trademark functions, it is possible nowadays to discern new ones, such as advertising and investing.[293] However, to the extent that functions serve to widen the protection afforded to trademarks,[294] they appear to merge into one another.

5.3.3.1 Guarantee of Origin

The most important function of a trademark is to enable consumers to distinguish one good from another.[295] Thus, a trademark aims at identifying a good as satisfactory to increase purchases by the consumer.[296] It creates goodwill by imprinting in the public perception a guarantee of constant and unique satisfaction that eventually (re)sells the good.[297] Thus, the effectiveness of a trademark's selling power is directly proportional to its degree of distinctiveness. Unsurprisingly, the goodwill function of marks has been mentioned alongside their origin function,

291 Peukert, p. 244.

292 WIPO Handbook, para. 2.330.

293 For an historical development of the functions of a trademark *see*: Neil Wilkof/ Daniel Burkitt, Trade Mark Licensing, 2nd ed., Sweet & Maxwell 2005, paras. 2.02–2.30 [Wilkof/Burkitt].

294 Wilkof/Burkitt, paras. 2.02–2.04.

295 Peter Groves (ed), Sourcebook on Intellectual Property Law, Cavendish Publishing 1997, p. 515 [Groves].

296 Groves, p. 515.

297 Groves, p. 516.

given that relevant subjective characteristics such as image, allure and aura constitute the main elements of communication between trademark owners and consumers.

In this sense, Frank Schechter identified four main principles arising out of the theory of origin:[298] (1) the value of trademarks lies in their selling power and so must be afforded sufficient protection; (2) the selling power of a trademark is determined by consumers' perception of the merits, uniqueness and singularity of the goods; (3) the distinctiveness of a trademark is affected by its use in related and non-related products; and (4) the degree of afforded protection depends on the actual differentiation from other marks.[299] Accordingly, the main rationale behind trademark protection is triggered by the need to preserve the distinctive function of a mark,[300] so as to ensure that consumers will repeat their purchase choices in cases where they are able to associate a given mark with a satisfactory product.

5.3.3.2 Guarantee of Quality

Along the same lines, the guarantee of quality function refers to trademarks as identified satisfactory sources that increase the selling power of the goods bearing them.[301] Thus, the underlying assumption is that consumers, based on previous satisfactory experiences, will consider all goods bearing a particular trademark as being of high quality.[302] Hence, the functional distinction between origin and quality becomes rather superfluous.

Notwithstanding the apparent futility of this classification, it is argued that the quality function of trademarks is of an economic rather than a legal nature and therefore, its legal protection is rarely guaranteed through enforcement mechanisms. Trademark owners are not legally bound to offer a constant level of quality in the goods bearing the mark.

298 FRANK I. SCHECHTER, 'The Rational Basis of Trademark Protection' (1926) 40 Harvard Law Review, pp. 813–833 [SCHECHTER].

299 SCHECHTER, p. 1927.

300 Although almost a century old, SCHECHTER's theory remains up-to-date: WILLIAM LANDES/RICHARD POSNER, The Economic Structure of Intellectual Property Law, Harvard University Press 2003, p. 167 [LANDES/POSNER].

301 LANDES/POSNER, p. 167.

302 LANDES/POSNER, p. 167.

As a result, the risk of conveying misleading information will increase. Consumers will tend to purchase a good bearing a mark that they can associate with previous good experiences, effectively without knowing whether that product complies with the high standards it used to. Consequently, the quality function of a trademark *de facto* imposes a higher standard of compliance on its owner. Any failure to reach this threshold would lead to a loss of distinction and thus, of consumer trust.

5.4 The Legal Framework for Trademarks under the TRIPS Agreement

The TRIPS Agreement provides a framework to protect the rights of trademark holders against third parties.[303] Article 15 of the TRIPS Agreement defines the concept of a trademark, while Article 16 established the rights conferred to trademark owners. The exceptions to the rights conferred are found in Article 17 of the TRIPS Agreement. Relevant in assessing the legality of food labelling standards is Article 20 of the TRIPS Agreement, which lays down specific requirements for exceptions to trademark rights.

5.4.1 The Definition of a Trademark

Article 15.1 of the TRIPS Agreement provides a uniform, international definition of a trademark for goods and services.[304] It reads:

303 This Section is partly based on previous published work: MARIELA MAIDANA-ELETTI, 'Market Access and Trademark Protection in the WTO Regime: The Case of Certification Marks' in: LEA SCHLÄPFER/HELENA ZAUGG (eds), Recht und Gesundheit, Schulthess 2013, pp. 69–86.

304 PETER-TOBIAS STOLL/FRANK SCHORKOPF, WTO: World Economic Order, World Trade Law, Max Plank Institute for Comparative Public and International Law, Martinus Nijhoff Publishers 2003, para. 632; JAN SCHMIDT-PFITZNER, 'Article 15' in: PETER-TOBIAS STOLL/JAN BUSCHE/KATRIN AREND (eds), WTO – Trade Related Aspects of Intellectual Property Rights, Max Planck Commentaries on World

> Any sign, or any combination of signs, capable of distinguishing the goods or services of one undertaking from those of other undertakings, shall be capable of constituting a trademark. Such signs, in particular words including personal names, letters, numerals, figurative elements and combinations of colours as well as any combination of such signs, shall be eligible for registration as trademarks. Where signs are not inherently capable of distinguishing the relevant goods or services, Members may make registrability depend on distinctiveness acquired through use. Members may require, as a condition of registration, that signs be visually perceptible.

This provision aims at harmonising the diversity of concepts found in divergent national legislation regarding the scope of protection and the registration requirements.[305] Without entering the debate about trademarks as property, which has been already extensively dealt with in academic literature,[306] the following section describes the characteristics and functions of trademarks in the light of the TRIPS Agreement.

5.4.1.1 The Characteristics of a Trademark

Signs are protectable as a trademark as long as they possess an abstract capability to distinguish those goods produced by one business from those produced by other businesses.[307] Furthermore, the capability requirement must be fulfilled for a trademark to be registered. It also provides an illustrative, non-exhaustive list of examples of signs eligible for registration.[308] The capability of a sign does not impose upon Members the obligation to register a given trademark. Quite to the contrary, Article 15.1 of the TRIPS Agreement allows Members to deny registration on the grounds provided for in the TRIPS Agreement and the Paris

---

Trade Law, Martinus Nijhoff Publishers 2009, pp. 306–316, p. 307 [SCHMIDT-PFINTZER].

305 SCHMIDT-PFINTZER, p. 307.

306 See *inter alia*: DANIEL GERVAIS, The TRIPS Agreement – Drafting History and Analysis, 3rd ed., Sweet & Maxwell 2008, p. 156 *et seq*.

307 For a critical view on the wording of Art. 15.1 of the TRIPS Agreement *see*: NUNO PIRES DE CARVAHLO, The TRIPS Regime of Trademarks and Designs, 2nd Ed., Kluwer Law International 2006, para. 15.8 [PIRES DE CARVAHLO].

308 SCHMIDT-PFINTZER, p. 307; PIRES DE CARVAHLO, para. 15.8.

Convention.[309] Furthermore, the TRIPS Agreement provides Members with a wide margin of discretion in adopting their own national conditions. As such, Members may register signs that are not inherently capable of distinguishing goods based on 'distinctiveness acquired through use'.[310] In addition, Members may deny the registration of signs that are not 'visually perceptive'.[311] The TRIPS Agreement also admits certain exceptions, and thus allows Members to make registration conditional upon use,[312] although actual use is not required for filing a registration.[313]

5.4.1.2 The Functions of a Trademark

As stated above, Article 15.1 of the TRIPS Agreement establishes that trademarks distinguish specific goods produced by one business from those goods produced by other businesses. Thus, it does not explicitly refer to the role of a trademark in distinguishing goods from the *same* business. However, this provision should be read in conjunction with Article 20 of the TRIPS Agreement, in as far as the latter implicitly includes the trademark function of distinguishing similar goods produced by the same business by referring to the 'trademark distinguishing the goods [...] in question of that undertaking'.[314] It follows that the differing approaches to the real function of a trademark[315] are both a legal compromise and a wider margin of discretion for domestic legislation.

The second function afforded to trademarks under the TRIPS Agreement refers to the capability of identifying the business producing the

309 This was the conclusion reached by the Appellate Body in *US – Section 211*, in which it was recognised that Members retain their right to adopt domestic legislation on the filing and registration of trademarks, provided they do not conflict with Art. 15.1 of the TRIPS Agreement.

310 Art. 15.1, sentence 3 of the TRIPS Agreement.

311 Art. 15.1, sentence 4 of the TRIPS Agreement.

312 Art. 15.3 of the TRIPS Agreement.

313 The common law user-based system approach and the civil law registration-based regime found a compromise in Art. 15.3 TRIPS Agreement. See *also*: Schmidt-Pfintzer, pp. 310–311.

314 For a detailed analysis of this interpretation *see*: Pires de Carvahlo, paras. 15.9–15.11.

315 See *e.g.*: GATT Report, *EC Draft TRIPS Agreement*, 29 March 1990, MTN.GNG/NG11/W/68 [*EC Draft TRIPS*]; and GATT Report, *US Draft TRIPS Agreement*, 11 May 1990, MTN.GNG/NG11/W70.

goods. This function corresponds with the wording of Article 20, which refers to the use of trademarks that identify the business producing the goods. However, caution is advised in accepting this function as an inherent one to trademarks due to the high risk of confusion with the function of trade names.[316]

5.4.2 Trademark Rights Conferred

5.4.2.1 A Presumption of Absoluteness

A minimum standard of protection for trademark owners is established in Article 16.1 of the TRIPS Agreement. This provision reads:

> The owner of a registered trademark shall have the exclusive right to prevent all third parties not having the owner's consent from using in the course of trade identical or similar signs for goods or services which are identical or similar to those in respect of which the trademark is registered where such use would result in a likelihood of confusion [...].

Based on this wording, however, it is disputed whether the exclusive nature of trademark rights is absolute. In principle, the right to use a given sign in the course of trade results from economic freedom rather than from intellectual property law.[317] In fact, the legislative history of the TRIPS Agreement shows that it was only in the second phase of the negotiations that the Members agreed to emphasise the negative or exclusive aspects of trademark rights.[318] As is the case with Article 15, the wording of Article 16.1 TRIPS Agreement should be interpreted in the light of the positive use of trademark rights enshrined in its Article 20. Likewise, the exclusive right of trademark owners to prohibit third parties from using signs conflicting with their own trademark must be analysed in conjunction with the rights granted to trademark

316 In order to avoid overlapping with other TRIPS provisions, the function referred to here should be understood as, '*used as an indication of source*.' For a critical explanation *see*: Pires de Carvahlo, para. 15.11.

317 Pires de Carvahlo, para. 16.1.

318 *EC Draft TRIPS*, p. 5.

owners by means of the exceptions listed in Article 17 of the TRIPS Agreement.[319]

5.4.2.2 Protection against Confusion

The likelihood of confusion test serves the purpose of determining whether the use of a mark similar to a registered mark is capable of distinguishing those goods. This test arises out of the trademark owners' right to prevent third parties from using similar signs in order to preserve the distinctiveness of their own trademark and in consequence, to avoid confusion. Conversely, the concept defining 'likeliness of confusion' has not been defined within the TRIPS Agreement, and therefore it is for the national legal systems and practices of Members to determine whether this threshold has a narrower or wider meaning.[320] It follows that members may grant trademark protection according to the degree of distinctiveness present in the registered mark. In fact, Article 16.1 of the TRIPS Agreement attributes rights to prevent the use of a mark that would otherwise result in a situation where there is a likelihood of confusion. Hence, in cases where an absolute presumption of likelihood has been established between identical marks and identical goods, Article 16.1 of the TRIPS Agreement is infringed. In other words, the presumption of infringement is not alleviated in the sense that the burden of proof will then fall on the claimant and, unlike the case with patents, it does not allow proof to the contrary.[321] Consequently, the likelihood of confusion threshold for trademarks within TRIPS appears to be lower than that imposed for other intellectual property rights.[322]

319 It has been argued that the mere existence of a legitimate interest creates a presumption of entitlement: Pires de Carvahlo, para. 16.6.

320 For instance, while '*likelihood of confusion*' refers to individual consumers, '*misleading the public*' would have a more general connotation, and refers to the public at large. For an explanation on the different approaches *see*: Pires de Carvahlo, para. 16.9.

321 Pires de Carvahlo, para. 16.11.

322 See *e.g.* Art. 34.1 of the TRIPS Agreement, which establishes the prevalence of the presumption only in the absence of proof to the contrary.

5.4.3 Exceptions to the Trademark Rights

The rights granted to trademark owners are limited by the exception set out in Article 17 of the TRIPS Agreement. It establishes that:

> Members may provide limited exceptions to the rights conferred by a trademark, such as fair use of descriptive terms, provided that such exceptions take account of the legitimate interests of the owner of the trademark and of third parties.

Thus, the trademark exception aims at preventing others from using signs similar or identical to the registered mark.[323] Similar to the application of Article XX GATT,[324] a measure that is inconsistent with Article 16 of the TRIPS Agreement may still qualify as a limited exception under Article 17. Hence, this provision legitimises domestic legislation that imposes limitations on trademark rights in that it provides a legal framework for exceptions.[325] It features a number of conditions that a limiting measure has to meet in order to be TRIPS-consistent. The origin of this threshold dates from the Review Conference of the Berne Convention[326] in 1967, where Article 9(2) was introduced. This clause aims at controlling the legality of exceptions to the rights conferred to the reproduction of works. It is written using flexible wording that allows for a compromise between common and civil law systems. As such, the *numerous clausus* exceptions preferred by continental law and the doctrine of fair use mostly followed in common law systems can find breathing space to best adapt to the needs of their own frameworks.[327]

Article 17 was interpreted by the Panel in EC-Trademarks,[328] whereby a three-step test for exceptions was established, requiring them to be limited and to take into account the legitimate interests of the trademark owners and the interests of third parties.

323 Pires de Carvahlo, para. 17.2.
324 See *supra*, Chapter 2, Section IV.
325 Pires de Carvahlo, para. 17.4.
326 Berne Covention for the Protection of Literary and Artistic Works, above.
327 Edson Beas Rodriguez Jr., The General Exceptions Clauses of the TRIPS Agreement: Promoting Sustainable Development, Cambridge University Press 2012, p. 19 [Rodriguez].
328 *EC – Trademarks*, paras. 7.644–7.688.

5.4.3.1 Notion of Limited Exceptions

The Panel decided to interpret Article 17 of the TRIPS Agreement restrictively to the extent that it would not undercut the body of rules from which it was made.[329] After referring to the common shared elements found in the copyright and patents exceptions found in Articles 13 and 30 of the TRIPS Agreement respectively, the Panel concluded that Article 17 TRIPS should nevertheless be interpreted in its own terms. In other words, a measure that qualifies as a limited exception will be consistent with the TRIPS Agreement in as far as it does not render the minimum standard of protection afforded or the rights conferred to trademark owners void of meaning. Unlike the wide margin of interpretation applied in cases involving general exception under Article XX GATT, the general approach taken by the Panel in construing Article 17 of the TRIPS Agreement is that of a narrow connotation.[330]

5.4.3.1.1 Fair Use of Descriptive Terms

The inclusion of the illustrative example 'fair use of descriptive terms' as a justified exception in Article 17 has triggered a considerable amount of debate.[331] Consequently, the Panel provided in EC – Trademarks an explanation on the purpose of this text.[332] It can be inferred from its findings that this illustrative element contains three main elements.[333] First, the use of descriptive terms may qualify as a limited exception in so far as they refer to the use of protected trademarks by third parties to describe goods, and not to descriptive marks, which do not fall within the scope of trademark protection due to their lack of distinctiveness.[334] *Argumentum e contrario*, descriptive marks that have acquired a secondary meaning, and thus fall under Article 16(1) may constitute a descriptive term in the

329 *EC – Trademarks*, paras. 6.644–6.661.

330 *EC – Trademarks*, para. 7.650.

331 See, *inter alia*, Pires de Carvahlo, paras. 17.10–17.16; for a detailed description of the term and its evolution in the US system *see*: Lisa Ramsey, 'Descriptive Trademarks and the First Amendment' (2005) 10 Tennessee Law Review, pp. 1110–1121; Margreth Barret, 'Reconciling Fair Use and Trademark Use' (2010) 28 (1) Cardozo Arts & Entertainment, pp. 1–63.

332 *EC – Trademarks*, para. 7.654.

333 Pires de Carvahlo, para. 17.11.

334 Pires de Carvahlo, para. 17.12; Rodriguez, p. 110.

sense of Article 17 TRIPS. As a result of this, trademark owners cannot oppose third parties' fair use of their trademarks to describe goods or services. Second, the use of the descriptive term must be fair in that it does not tarnish the reputation of the mark or reduce its distinctiveness. Therefore, third parties may use protected trademarks for purposes of promotion, such as distributors and retailers, provided that no harm to the reputation and degree of distinctiveness is guaranteed.[335] Third, the fair use of descriptive terms constitutes a limitation *per se*, because it provides *a priori* interpretative guidance of possible justified limited exceptions. Excluding the illustrative example given by Article 17 in interpreting the existence of a limited exception would lead to a manifestly incorrect result.[336] Indeed, the expression 'fair use of descriptive terms' is a shortcut to describe a weaker trademark that, although still entitled to IP protection due to its distinctive character, is subject to a lesser degree of exclusivity as a result of customary practices of trade.[337] Thus, the qualitative characteristic of an exception is the determinant factor in carrying out an assessment of the likelihood of confusion.

5.4.3.2 Legitimate Interests of the Owner

The meaning of the second condition for a justified exception leaves no space for ambivalent interpretation after the clear wording of the Panel in *EC – Trademarks*, whereby it stated that 'legitimate interests' are understood as normative claim calling for the protection of justifiable interests backed by relevant public policies and other social norms.[338] It distinguishes between the legitimate interests of trademark owners and the rights conferred by a trademark, concluding that the latter should not be confused with the enjoyment of legal rights. The Panel succeeded in identifying the economic value of a mark, its reputation and quality as legitimate interests within the meaning of Article 17 of the TRIPS Agreement.[339] It follows from the non-exhaustive nature of the rights conferred to trademark owners in Article 16.1 of the TRIPS Agreement

335 Pires de Carvahlo, para. 17.13–17.14; Rodriguez, p. 110.

336 *EC – Trademarks*, para. 7.648; Rodriguez, p. 110.

337 Pires de Carvahlo, para. 17.12.

338 *EC – Trademarks*, para. 7.662.

339 *EC – Trademarks*, para. 7.664.

that their legitimate interests go beyond those rights stemming from the use of a mark in the course of trade, as they also encompass the rights arising from the unauthorised use of a mark outside the course of trade. Equally, the mere existence of a legitimate interest will give rise to a right to defend those interests. The broader scope given to the concept of 'legitimate interest' serves the purpose of enabling trademark owners to protect their exclusive rights from possible collateral infringements as a result of social norms and public policy measures.

5.4.3.3 Lesser Standard of Regard for the Interests of Third Parties

The third step of the test refers to the consideration of third party interests. The Panel identified as legitimate the interest of consumers in being able to distinguish goods from different businesses to avoid confusion.[340] The expression 'third parties' refers not only to consumers, but also to trademark licensees and persons using a geographical indication in accordance with a geographical indication registration.[341] Additionally, the Panel acknowledged that the expression 'take account of'[342] suggests a lesser standard of regard for the interests of trademark owners and third parties when compared to the wording used for the exceptions found in Articles 13 and 30 of the TRIPS Agreement.

5.4.4 Special Trademark Requirements

Article 20 of the TRIPS Agreement refers to other special requirements that may affect the use of a trademark during the course of trade. It reads:

> The use of a trademark in the course of trade shall not be unjustifiably encumbered by special requirements, such as use with another trademark, use in a special form or use in a manner detrimental to its capability to distinguish the goods or services of one undertaking from those of other undertakings. This will not preclude a requirement prescribing the use of the trademark identifying the undertaking producing the goods or services along with, but without linking it to, the trademark distinguishing the goods or services in question of that undertaking.

340 *EC – Trademarks*, para. 7.676.

341 *EC – Trademarks*, paras. 7.680-1.

342 *EC – Trademarks*, para. 7.671, referring to '*unreasonable prejudice*'.

It applies in cases of goods bearing a mark that is allowed to be placed onto a given market upon fulfilment of special domestic requirements. In particular, it imposes upon Members the duty to refrain from requiring foreigners to link their marks to those of local producers. Hence, the autonomy of Members to legislate on marks is thereby considerably reduced.[343] It thus follows that one of the unintended effects of Article 20 TRIPS is a loss of distinctiveness by means of the governmental imposition of encumbrances on the use of marks.[344]

Given that avoidance of confusion is deemed a legitimate interest of the trademark owner in the light of Article 17, the need for governments to take account of those interests appears unavoidable.[345] However, the three-step test will not find application in cases where the encumbrances are justified. Whether the adopted special measures constitute a curtailment to the exclusive rights of trademark owners that fall within the meaning of a limited exception in the sense of Article 17 will be irrelevant in cases where Article 20 applies, because only a proportionality assessment will be required to establish compliance with the TRIPS Agreement. Thus, the threshold imposed by Article 20 through a proportionality test is considerably lower than that imposed by the three-step test in Article 17.

In the light of the interpretation given by the Panel in *Indonesia – Autos*[346] it is worth noting that special requirements accepted voluntarily and in the knowledge of any consequent implications for the ability to use a pre-existing trademark by a (foreign) trademark owner as a condition for the obtainment of certain privileges, do not fall within the scope of Article 20 TRIPS.[347] Hence, caution must be exercised in granting benefits to certain domestic producers in order to avoid an unfair competitive advantage over foreign ones.[348] Although voluntary in nature, compliance

343 Graeme Dinwoodie/Rochelle Dreyfuss, A Neofederalist Vision of TRIPS: The Resilience of the International Intellectual Property Regime, Oxford University Press 2012, p. 36.

344 Pires de Carvahlo, para. 20.22.

345 Pires de Carvahlo, para. 20.22.

346 *Indonesia – Autos*, para. 14.270–14.276.

347 *Indonesia – Autos*, para. 14.276.

348 *Indonesia – Autos*, para. 14.273.

with special (domestic) requirements may constitute a *de facto* trade barrier that hinders the effective access of foreign products to the domestic market.

5.5 Conclusion

Consumer and market demands have long played an essential role in triggering the proliferation of food labelling standards because their purpose is to indicate that foodstuffs are of a certain origin, material, and quality. It becomes apparent why food labelling standards under the protection of trademark law can become a *de facto* obstacle to market access.

Section II examined how the conflict between exclusive trademark rights and consumer protection has its origins in incepted dynamics well preceding the establishment of the WTO. It showed that the adoption of the TRIPS Agreement was largely motivated by the desire to avoid trade-distorting behaviour stemming from widely differing standards of protection and enforcement of intellectual property rights.

Section III explained what trademarks are and why they are important for international trade in food. In doing so, it defined trademarks according to the principles of International Intellectual Property Law, while at the same time providing a taxonomy to facilitate the legal analysis. It also examined the two main functions of trademarks: guarantee of origin and, more importantly for this work, guarantee of quality.

Section IV examined the legal framework applicable to trademarks in WTO Law. It first determined what constituted a trademark, analysing the peculiarities of its characteristics and functions under Article 15.1 of the TRIPS Agreement. The analysis then focused on the rights conferred to trademark owners, their attributed presumption of absoluteness, as well as the protection afforded against confusion under Article 16.1 of the TRIPS Agreement. The exceptions to these conferred trademark rights were scrutinised in the light of Article 17 and its interpretative jurisprudence, whereby a three-tier compliance test was developed. A measure will fall under the exception of Article 17 of the TRIPS Agreement if it is of a limited nature or if it takes into account the legitimate interests of trademark holders and the interests of third parties. Lastly, this section analysed the special trademark requirements under Article 20 of the TRIPS Agreement, concluding that the threshold established therein is considerably lower than that provided in the limited exceptions clause of Article 17.

Before concluding, and as a mode of illustrative example, section V presented a case study at the intersection between food labelling standards and WTO Law by examining Australia's plain packaging scheme for tobacco products. It argued that plain packaging does not affect the rights conferred to trademark owners under Article 16.1, nor does it breach Article 20 of the TRIPS Agreement.

The previous chapter analysed the implications of the TRIPS Agreement in the construction of new forms of food governance. The next chapter will turn our focus to the role of the SPS Agreement within the wider context of international food standards.

6. Food Safety Standards as Sanitary and Phytosanitary Measures

6.1 Health Protection and Food Safety

The protection of human, animal and plant life and health has always been one of the main objectives of government regulation. However, due to the consolidation of the modern welfare state in developed countries, as well as the increasingly important role of the media in food scares, an increase in the adoption of health and safety regulation was identified during the first decade of the 21st century.[349] Although the protection of public health, understood as a concept that develops alongside consumers' perception of it in a given country, remains a legitimate aim to adopt regulation, these efforts often result in 'a virtual minefield for trade policy makers',[350] where international trade rules and domestic standards collide.

As such, differing food safety standards arising out of different regulatory approaches impose important non-tariff barriers to trade. This regulatory diversity, albeit legitimate, poses serious challenges to the free flow of trade in foodstuffs. The exploitation of these regulatory differences is legitimate enough to leverage trade-distorting behaviour, whereby regulation is understood as a way of allocating (market) power. Differing minimum food safety standards, however, constitutes one of the main hurdles in guaranteeing global market access.

349 Michael Trebilcock/Julie Soloway, 'International Trade Policy and Domestic Food Safety Regulation: The Case for Substantial Deference by the WTO Dispute Settlement Body under the SPS Agreement' in: Daniel Kennedy/James Southwick (eds), The Political Economy of International Trade Law, Essays in Honor of Robert E. Hudec, Cambridge University Press 2002, pp. 537–574, p. 538 [Trebilcock/Soloway]. See *also*: Joanne Scott, Commentary on the Sanitary and Phytosanitary Measures Agreement, Oxford University Press 2007.

350 Trebilcock/Soloway, p. 537.

While it is clear that different regulatory food safety regimes enhance the benefits of comparative advantage, efforts to level the playing field through legal harmonisation are at times superfluous and can be quickly rendered void of meaning.

Although the minimum standard of public health protection has traditionally fallen within the realm of sovereign states,[351] new forms of governance have been developed in the last two decades. The growing development of a new legal architecture for global food governance has not only led to the creation of new rules governing food quality, but also those applying specifically to food safety. Since the establishment of the WTO, the SPS Agreement remains the most important legal instrument in matters of trade in safe food.[352]

This chapter starts with a brief overview of the historical development of the SPS Agreement. It later examines the definition of an SPS measure under WTO law. Section IV concentrates on the relevant SPS principles for trade in food. In doing so, it will examine the role of international standards and harmonising efforts, the obligation to base SPS measures on science and the rationale underlying the precautionary principle. The importance given to the principle of equivalence or mutual recognition will be addressed in this section too. Section V offers a case study on the widely disputed use of private food safety standards in international trade. Section VI will briefly conclude.

6.2 The SPS Agreement in Context

The genesis of the SPS Agreement can be tracked back to the Tokyo Standards Code Agreement of 1979. A sub-category of measures related

351 For example, the SPS Agreement does not impose upon Members the obligation to adopt a particular level of protection, which remains a matters of national authority; *Australia – Salmon*, para. 199.

352 Discussing the lack of an appropriate international legal instrument to test sanitary and phytosanitary measures prior to the adoption of the SPS Agreement *see*: THOMAS COTTIER, 'Risk Management Experience in WTO Dispute Settlement' in: DAVID ROBERTSON/AYNSLEY KELLOW (eds), Globalization and the Environment: Risk Assessment in the WTO, Edward Elgar 2011, pp. 41–62.

to food safety, animal and plant life and health was also included.[353] However, the impact of this inclusion in the regulatory approaches of GATT members was rather limited. In fact, no single SPS measure was successfully challenged in the GATT dispute settlement system.[354] Concerns about the increasing recourse to SPS measures after the liberalisation of the markets for agricultural products were voiced from the beginning of the Uruguay Round negotiations.[355] Although initially the SPS negotiations took place within the general discussions on agriculture, an individual working group on SPS measures was formed by 1988. A draft text of what is now known as the SPS Agreement was produced two years later.[356] As such, the SPS Agreement aims at improving human, animal and plant life and health in all Members[357] while minimising the negative trade effect of SPS measures and promoting international trade.[358] Although Members retain their right to choose their own adequate level of SPS protection,[359] the SPS Agreement provides a legal backdrop to assess whether those national SPS measures constitute disguised barriers to trade.

353 David Wirth, 'The Role of Science in the Uruguay Round and NAFTA Trade Disciplines' (1994) 27 Cornell International Law Journal, pp. 817–859.

354 Lucasz Gruszczynski, Regulating Health and Environmental Risks under WTO Law: A Critical Analysis of the SPS Agreement, Oxford University Press 2010, p. 36 [Gruszczynski].

355 GATT, Ministerial Declaration on the Uruguay Round (Punta del Este Declaration), 20 September 1986, BISD 33S/19 (1987). See *also*: Denise Prévost/Peter Van den Bossche, The Agreement on the Application of Sanitary and Phytosanitary Measures, in: Patrick Macrory/Arthur Appleton/Michael Plummer (eds), The World Trade Organization: Legal, Economic and Political Analysis, Springer 2005, pp. 239–244.

356 Gruszczynski, p. 37.

357 Preamble to the SPS Agreement, recital 1.

358 *EC – Hormones*, para. 177.

359 Annex A, para. 5 of the SPS Agreement states that the appropriate level of sanitary or phytosanitary protection is the level of protection deemed appropriate by the Member establishing that sanitary or phytosanitary measures to protect human, animal or plant life or health within its territory.

6.3 What is an SPS Measure?

The SPS Agreement, in its Annex 1.A,[360] defines SPS measures as any measure applied:

- 'to protect animal or plant life or health within the territory of the Member from risks arising from the entry, establishment, or spread of pests, diseases, disease-carrying organisms, or disease-causing organisms;
- to protect human or animal life or health within the territory of the Member from risks arising from additives, contaminants, toxins or disease-causing organisms in foods, beverages or feedstuffs;
- to protect human life or health within the territory of the Member from risks arising from diseases carried by animals, plants or products thereof, or from the entry, establishment or spread of pests; or
- to prevent or limit any other damage within the territory of the Member from entry, establishment or spread of pests'.

Due to the wide array of possible SPS measures, it is important to identify categories of situations where they may constitute non-tariff trade barriers and thus violate WTO rules.[361] These categories include the prohibition of the sale of an imported product on health grounds,[362] positive requirements for imported products that discriminate against foreign products, the exclusion of imported products from pre-market approval schemes and compliance with voluntary standards. Thus, Members may adopt SPS measures that are necessary to the extent that they comply with the different provisions of the SPS Agreement.[363] They must

360 STEVEN CHARNOVITZ, 'Article 1 and Annex A SPS' in: RÜDIGER WOLFRUM/PETER-TOBIAS STOLL/ANJA SEIBERT-FOHR (eds), WTO-Technical Barriers and SPS Measures, Volume III, Martinus Nijhoff Publishers 2007, pp. 375–391.

361 These categories were first developed by SYKES in Product Standards 1995, p. 17. They were later built upon by TRACEY EPPS, in: International Trade and Health Protection: A Critical Assessment of the WTO's SPS Agreement, Edward Elgar 2008, p. 12 [EPPS].

362 *EC – Hormones*; WTO, Appellate Body Report, Japan – Measures Affecting the Importation of Apples, 23 November 2003, WT/DS245/AB/R [*Japan – Apples*].

363 Art. 2.1 of the SPS Agreement.

be based on scientific principles and may not be maintained without scientific evidence, except in cases where the precautionary principle under Article 5.7 of the SPS Agreement applies.[364]

Furthermore, any SPS measure must also comply with the principle of non-discrimination. This pillar of WTO Law, as explained in chapter 1, is also found in Article 2.3 of the SPS Agreement and ensures that Members do not impose SPS measures that arbitrarily or unjustifiably discriminate against other Members where identical or similar conditions prevail (like products). Likewise, SPS measures must not be applied in a trade-distorting manner. While determining the appropriate SPS measure, Members must take into account the potential economic damage in terms of loss of production or sales in the event of entry, establishment or spread of pests or diseases, the costs of their control or eradication in the territory of the importing Member and the relative cost-effectiveness of alternative approaches to limit these risks.[365]

6.4 Relevant SPS Principles for Food Standards

6.4.1 International Standards and Harmonisation

One of the most significant contributions to the increased importance of international standards is found in Article 3.1 of the SPS Agreement. This provision imposes an obligation on Members to base their SPS measures on international standards, guidelines and recommendations, where they exist. As a result, a presumption of compliance with the SPS Agreement will exist in cases where an SPS measure is based on an international standard.[366] However, this minimum threshold of protection does not prevent Members from adopting higher standards of protection that those stipulated on the relevant international standard, provided sufficient scientific justification is available.[367]

364 Art. 2.2 of the SPS Agreement. See *infra*, Section IV.
365 Art. 5.3 of the SPS Agreement.
366 Art. 3.2 of the SPS Agreement.
367 Art. 3.3 of the SPS Agreement.

Article 3.3 of the SPS Agreement, however, allows WTO Members to opt out of compliance with international standards in cases where the following requirements are fulfilled: the measures adopted are science-based; a risk assessment is carried out in cases where the measure deviates from international standards; and the measure applies only to the necessary extent to protect human, animal or plant life or health. In cases where this provision is called upon, Members are obliged to notify these measures prior to implementation.

Article 3.4 of the SPS Agreement also imposes upon Members the obligation to participate within their resources in the relevant international standard-setting bodies, particularly the CAC, the IPPC and the OIE.[368] This is translated in the notification procedure put in place by the SPS Agreement. In fact, the growth of these notifications proves the increased relevance of international standards. To put it into perspective, the Committee on Sanitary and Phytosanitary Measures received between January 2009 and March 2011 a total of 1,861 regular notifications of SPS measures. Measures based on a relevant international standard amounted to 40 per cent of the notifications.[369] In those measures identified as being based on a relevant international standard, 53 per cent related to the CAC, 27 per cent to the IPPC and 20 per cent to OIE standard.[370]

The role of international standards increases in emergency situations. Members have shown the tendency to adopt emergency SPS measures mainly based on the relevant international standards. During the same period of time as identified above, the SPS Committee received a total of 399 emergency notifications. The existence of a relevant international standard was indicated in 333 cases.[371]

The rationale behind the divergent numbers between regular and emergency SPS measures based on relevant international standards can be explained by referring to the decision-making process on domestic levels. While lengthy legislative processes may delay the modification of national legislation in order to implement new relevant international

368 See *supra*, Chapter 3 on Standard-Setting Organisations.

369 Committee on Sanitary and Phytosanitary Measures, Monitoring the Use of International Standards, 30 May 2011, G/SPS/GEN/1086, para. 5 [SPS Committee, Monitoring the Use of International Standards].

370 SPS Committee, Monitoring the Use of International Standards 2011, para. 6.

371 SPS Committee, Monitoring the Use of International Standards 2011, para. 11.

standards, emergency situations lend themselves well as a catalyst to level the regulatory level playing field.

6.4.2 *Scientific Basis and the Precautionary Principle*

Members must ensure that their SPS measures are based on an assessment of the risks to human, animal or plant life or health, taking into account risk assessment techniques developed by the relevant international organisations.[372]

Risk assessment has been defined in Annex A.4 of the SPS Agreement as the evaluation of the likelihood of entry, establishment or spread of a pest or disease within the territory of an importing Member and of the associated potential biological and economic consequences. It also refers to the evaluation of the potential for adverse effects on human or animal health arising from the presence of additives, contaminants, toxins or disease-causing organisms in food, beverages, or animal feed.

Therefore, risk assessment within the meaning of Article 5.1 of the SPS Agreement must:

- identify the diseases whose entry, establishment or spread a Member wants to prevent within its territory, as well as the potential biological and economic consequences associated with the entry, establishment or spread of these diseases;
- evaluate the likelihood of entry, establishment or spread of these diseases, as well as the associated potential biological and economic consequences; and
- evaluate the likelihood of entry, establishment or spread of these diseases according to the SPS measures which might be applied.[373]

Equally, Members may request from another Member maintaining an SPS measure based on the precautionary principle an explanation of the reasons for the adoption of such a measure, if that measure is

372 Art. 5.1 of the SPS Agreement.
373 *Australia – Salmon*, para. 121.

constraining or has the potential to constrain trade and no relevant international standards exist.[374]

For example, in *EC – Hormones*, the European Union had adopted an SPS measure based on Article 5.7 that prohibited the sale of American and Canadian hormone-fed beef. Although there was little scientific evidence for the ban, the EU argued that it constituted a legitimate response to public concerns about the carcinogenic effects of hormones used as growth stimulants. Five out of six of the growth hormone used by the US and Canada were the subject of CAC standards, and thus complied with relevant international standards.

One of the most significant findings of the Panel reports in this case is found in the reversal of proof, namely that the EU, by adopting more stringent standards, was obliged to justify the adopted SPS measure in accordance with Article 3.3 of the SPS Agreement.[375] The Appellate Body decided to reverse the Panel's findings.[376] It was of the opinion that the complainant Member still bears the burden of establishing a *prima facie* case for the allegedly trade-distorting SPS measure under other provisions of the SPS Agreement.

In *Australia – Salmon*, Canada challenged an SPS measure prohibiting the import of fresh, chilled and frozen salmon to Australia. The rationale behind this ban was to prevent the entry of any infectious or contagious disease affecting humans, animals or plants. As in EC – Hormones, the WTO Appellate Body found that the SPS measure failed to comply with the duty to carry out a risk assessment.[377] After these findings, Australia agreed to import Canadian salmon meeting domestic sanitary requirements.

In *Japan – Agriculture*, the US challenged a Japanese requirement to test the efficacy of quarantine treatments for a variety of certain agricultural products that translated into a separate approval for the import

374 Art. 5.8 of the SPS Agreement.

375 WTO Panel Report, *European Communities – Measures Concerning Meat and Meat Products (Hormones)*, 18 August 1997, WT/DS26/R/USA, para. 8.54 [*EC – Hormones*]; WTO Panel Report, *European Communities – Measures Concerning Meat and Meat Products (Hormones)*, 18 August 1997, WT/DS48/R/CAN, para. 8.57 [*EC – Hormones (Canada)*].

376 *EC – Hormones*, para. 104.

377 *Australia – Salmon*, para. 135.

of each variety of a particular fruit. Due to the lack of a risk assessment being carried out as a basis for these SPS measure, the WTO Panel and Appellate Body reports found the Japanese measure to be inconsistent with Article 5.7 of the SPS Agreement.[378]

In cases where scientific evidence is insufficient to justify an SPS measure, Article 5.7 provides for members to provisionally adopt them on the basis of available pertinent information. It is the obligation of the Member adopting an SPS measure based on the precautionary principle to obtain additional information in order to carry out a more objective risk assessment. Members are also obliged to review the adopted SPS measure within a reasonable period of time.

As established in *Japan – Agriculture*[379] and *Japan – Apples*,[380] four cumulative requirements must be fulfilled for a measure to be consistent with Article 5.7 of the SPS Agreement:

- the measure was imposed in respect of a situation where relevant scientific information is insufficient;
- the measure is based on the available pertinent information;
- the Member adopting the measure must seek to obtain the necessary additional information for a more objective assessment of risk;
- the Member adopting the measure must review it within a reasonable period of time.

The justification for this principle is found in the right of Members to address perceived or uncertain risks to public health before scientific answers that identify those risks become available to policy makers.

6.4.3 Mutual Recognition or Equivalence

Whereas an exporting Member is capable of objectively demonstrating that an adopted SPS measure complies with an importing Member's

378 WTO Appellate Body Report, *Japan – Measures Affecting Agricultural Products*, 19 March 1999, WT/DS76/AB/R, para. 85 *[Japan – Agriculture*].

379 *Japan – Agriculture*, para. 89.

380 *Japan – Apples*, para. 176.

appropriate level of sanitary and phytosanitary protection, Article 4.1 of the SPS Agreement imposes the obligation to accept such measures as equivalent. Similarly, Members must avoid arbitrary or unjustifiable distinctions in the levels of SPS protection they consider appropriate in different situations, if such distinctions result in discrimination or a disguised restriction on international trade. The adopted SPS measures shall not be more trade-restrictive than required to achieve the level of SPS protection considered as appropriate, taking into account technical and economic feasibility. A measure is deemed not to be more trade-restrictive than necessary unless there is another measure that achieves the same level of SPS protection that is significantly less restrictive to trade.[381]

In 2001, the SPS Committee issued a decision on the implementation of Article 4.1.[382] It detailed the necessary steps Members must follow to correctly implement this provision in their respective legal systems. This decision was revised on four subsequent occasions.

As its very essence, Article 4.1 provides a legal framework for the conclusion of further agreements on the recognition of SPS measures between trading partners,[383] while Article 4.2 encourages Members to inform the SPS Committee about their experiences implementing equivalence.[384] As one of the available regulatory approaches to reducing the trade-distorting effects of differing food standards, the principle of mutual recognition or equivalence has been particularly relevant in the formation of new forms of food governance.[385]

381 Art. 5.6 of the SPS Agreement.

382 Committee on Sanitary and Phytosanitary Measures, Decision on the Implementation of Article 4 of the SPS Agreement, 26 October 2001, G/SPS/19.

383 Epps, p. 125; Denise Prèvost/Peter van den Bossche, 'The Agreement on Sanitary and Phytosanitary Measures' in: Patrick Macrory/Arthur Appleton/Michael Plummer, The World Trade Organisation: Legal, Economic and Political Analysis, Springer 2005, pp. 231–370, p. 329.

384 Committee for Sanitary and Phytosanitary Measures, Equivalence: Consideration of Article 4 of the SPS Agreement, Summary of Informal Discussions on Equivalence, Second Report by the Chairman, 21 March 2001, SPS/G/L/445.

385 For a regional example between the EU and Switzerland see *infra*, Chapters 7 and 8.

6.5 Case Study: Private Food Safety Standards

The last decade has shown an increase in the use of standards solely designed and adopted by private players, and much has been written about the challenges they pose for international trade.[386] These standards are developed not by domestic policy-makers or international organisations, but are primarily designed by large supermarket chains in a bid to ensure the quality and safety of their retail products.[387] The contractual obligation to comply with a set of specific standards undoubtedly unfolds a binding effect from the private law perspective. In doing this, suppliers have to commit to a specified set of (food) standards in order to avoid breach of contract, and so it has been claimed that their voluntary nature becomes *de facto* mandatory.[388]

From a public international law perspective, however the proliferation of private voluntary food standards poses important challenges to the correct application of the WTO rules in particular. This is so due to the basic assumption that private parties, such as supermarket chains, are not subjects of international law and thus, obligations arising out of the Marrakesh Agreements do not apply to them. Jurisdictional objections

386 This section is partly based on previously published work: MARIELA MAIDANA-ELETTI, 'International Food Standards and WTO Law' (2014) 19 (2) Deakin Law Review, pp. 217–241; OECD, Final Report on Private Standards and the Shaping of Agro-Food Systems, Paris, Working Party on Agricultural Policies and Markets, 2006; see *also*: STEVE JAFFE/OLIVIER MASAKURE, 'Strategic Use of Private Standards to Enhance International Competitiveness: Vegetable Exports from Kenya and Elsewhere' (2005) 30 Food Policy, pp. 316–333; LINDA FULPONI, 'Private Standards Schemes and Developing Countries Access to Global Value Chains: Challenges and Opportunities Emerging from Four Case Studies' OECD, August 2007, AGR/CA/APM(2006)20/final [FULPONI]; TETTY HAVINGA, 'Private Regulation of Food Safety by Supermarkets' (2006) 28 (4) Law and Policy, pp. 515–533; LAWRENCE BUSCH, 'The Moral Economic of Grades and Standards' (2000) 16 Journal of Rural Studies, pp. 273–283 [BUSCH].

387 DORIS FUCHS/AGNI KALFAGIANNI/TETTY HAVINGA, Actors in Private Food Governance: The Legitimacy of Retail Standards and Multistakeholders Initiatives with Civil Society Prticipation, Agricultural Human Values, 2009 Springer [FUCHS *et al.*]

388 FUCHS *et al.*, p. 2; SPENCER HENSON/THOMAS REARDON, 'Private Agri-Food Standards: Implications for Food Policy and the Agri-Food System' (2005) 30 Food Policy, pp. 241–253.

aside, trade concerns about the implications of private parties imposing compliance with voluntary standards that go beyond the level of protection offered by domestic, WTO-compliant regulation in their cross-border contracts, have been raised in WTO fora. The question that remains open is whether the WTO Agreements, particularly the SPS Agreement, have sufficient flexibility to address the legal implications of private voluntary safety standards and so diminish the trade-distorting effects attributed to them.

6.5.1 Private Food Standard-Setting Entities

It has been claimed that this recent development has both positive and negative implications for international trade. They are trade-enhancing because they can contribute to product differentiation, improve quality and safety, disseminate modern and efficient technologies, and ultimately guarantee market access. They are trade-distorting because they disguise protectionist measures, artificially fragmentise markets, impose unreasonable requirements on suppliers, and thus restrict market access. Five key private standard-setting bodies have been identified as the major driving force behind the proliferation of private food safety standards: the Global Food Safety Initiative (GFSI), the Global Partnership for Good Agricultural Practices (GlobalGAP), Safe Quality Food (SQF), the International Food Standard (IFS) and the British Retail Consortium (BRC).

The GFSI was initiated in 2000 by a group of international retailers in order to agree on a globally accepted food safety benchmark. It sets baseline requirements for food safety standards and intends to improve efficiency costs throughout the food chain. Its central aim is to strengthen consumer confidence in food bought in retail outlets.[389]

GlobalGAP was first developed in 1997 as EurepGAP by a group of European retailers; since 2007 it has been known as GlobalGAP. It initially applied to fruit and vegetables only, but now also covers meat products and fish from aquaculture. Compliance with its standards requires the completion of a checklist consisting of 254 questions to obtain certification. SQF was developed in 1994 by the Western

389 Fuchs *et al.*, p. 3.

Australian Department of Agriculture and sold to the US in 2003. It is a food safety and quality program for primary production and for food manufacturing and distribution. It is now owned by the US Food Marketing Institute, whose membership represents three-quarters of American food retailers and 200 companies from over 50 countries.[390]

The IFS was initiated in 2002 by German food retailers. A year later the French food retailers association joined in, followed by the Italian Food Retailer Association. Retailers from Austria, Poland, Spain and Switzerland also adopted the IFS as their food safety standard. It deals with the processing of food and contains 250 requirements divided between production processes, management responsibility, quality management systems, resource management, measurements and improvements, as well as audit protocol.[391]

BRC was created in 1998 to evaluate the manufacturing of retailers' own brand products. It delineates more than 250 requirements including comprehensive norms for food safety and quality schemes, products and process management, and the personnel's personal hygiene.[392]

The number of what is considered private standard-setting entities continues to grow. While the line between entities embedded in public or private law is often blurred, this section does not attempt to examine the legal nature of the standard-setting entities. Rather, it focuses on the products produced, that is, the private food standard, which is currently under the scrutiny of the SPS Committee.

6.5.2 Discussions on Private Standards in the SPS Committee

These private voluntary food standards have raised concerns among governments of least developing and developing nations within the WTO. Although private food standards extend to both quality and safety, it is the latter which have received the most attention. In particular, the SPS Committee was called upon to establish a working group in order to

390 Fuchs *et al.*, p. 3.
391 Fuchs *et al.*, p. 3.
392 Fuchs *et al.*, p. 3.

tackle the issue of whether private safety standards fall within the scope of the SPS Agreement.

The first concerns were raised by St Vincent and the Grenadines in 2005, who complained about the additional requirements set by EurepGap for exporting bananas to the United Kingdom.[393] St Vincent and the Grenadines, supported, among others, by Ecuador[394] and Argentina,[395] complained that these additional private food standards are more stringent than the public mandatory food standards in place.

As a response to these concerns, the SPS Committee accorded to undertake a three-step comparative study on the effects of private SPS standards. As a first step, the Secretariat circulated a questionnaire about SPS-related private standards in 2008.[396] A second step saw the circulation in 2009 of a descriptive report summarising the information contained in the 40 responses obtained from 22 Members.[397] The Secretariat then prepared an analytical report identifying possible actions as the third and last step.[398] The proposed recommendations were amended after a discussion during the meetings of the *ad hoc* working group on private standards and the SPS Committee, and a revised version of the recommendations was circulated in March 2010.[399] After the *ad hoc* working

393 Committee on Sanitary and Phytosanitary Measures, Private Industry Standards, Communication from Saint Vincent and the Grenadines, 28 February 2007, G/SPS/GEN/766.

394 Committee on Sanitary and Phytosanitary Measures, Private and Commercial Standards: Statement by Ecuador at the Meeting of 27–28 June 2007, 5 July 2007, G/SPS/GEN/792.

395 Committee on Sanitary and Phytosanitary Measures, Private Standards and the SPS Agreement, Note of the Secretariat, 24 January 2007, G/SPS/W/246.

396 Committee on Sanitary and Phytosanitary Measures, Questionnaire on SPS-Related Private Standards, Note of the Secretariat, 8 December 2008, G/SPS/W/232.

397 Committee on Sanitary and Phytosanitary Measures, Effects of SPS-Related Private Standards: Descriptive Report, Note of the Secretariat, 15 June 2009, G/SPS/GEN/932.

398 Committee on Sanitary and Phytosanitary Measures, Possible Actions for the SPS Committee Regarding Private SPS Standards, Note of the Secretariat, 20 October 2009, G/SPS/W/247.

399 Committee on Sanitary and Phytosanitary Measures, Possible Actions for the SPS Committee regarding Private SPS Standards, 5 March 2010, G/SPS/W/247/Rev.1.

group meeting, a second revised version of the recommendations was circulated.[400] A couple of months later, a third revision of the recommendation was issued.[401]

In March 2011, six actions were proposed by the *ad hoc* working group on SPS-related private standards to the SPS Committee.[402] At its meeting on 20–31 March 2011, the SPS Committee adopted five of the six actions put forward:[403]

- **Action 1**: the SPS Committee should develop a working definition of SPS-related private standards and limit any discussions to these.
- **Action 2**: the SPS Committee should regularly inform Codex, OIE and IPPC regarding relevant developments in its considerations of SPS-related private standards, and should invite these organisations to likewise regularly inform the SPS Committee of relevant developments in their respective bodies.
- **Action 3**: The SPS Committee invites the Secretariat to inform the Committee on developments in other WTO business which could be of relevance for its discussions on SPS-related private standards.
- **Action 4**: Members are encouraged to communicate with entities involved in SPS-related private standards in their territories to sensitise them to the issues raised in the SPS Committee and underline the importance of international standards by the Codex, OIE and IPPC.
- **Action 5**: The SPS Committee should explore the possibility of working with the Codex, OIE and IPPC to support the development and/or dissemination of informative materials underlining the importance of SPS standards.

400 Committee on Sanitary and Phytosanitary Measures, Possible Actions for the SPS Committee Regarding SPS-Related Private Standards, Note by the Secretariat, 15 June 2010, G/SPS/W/247/Rev.2.

401 Committee on Sanitary and Phytosanitary Measures, Possible Actions for the SPS Committee Regarding SPS-Related Private Standards, Note by the Secretariat, 11 October 2010, G/SPS/W/247/Rev.3.

402 Committee on Sanitary and Phytosanitary Measures, Report of the *ad hoc* Working Group on SPS-Related Private Standards to the SPS Committee, 3 March 2011, G/SPS/W/256.

403 Committee on Sanitary and Phytosanitary Measures, Actions Regarding SPS-Related Private Standards, Decision of the Committee, 6 April 2011, G/SPS/55.

Since then, the SPS Committee has been working on addressing Action 1, namely establishing a working definition of SPS-related private standards.[404] As of June 2015, Members remain deadlocked. Although New Zealand and China – as co-stewards of the working group – have managed to present a draft definition of private SPS standards,[405] consensus among Members was not reached and a 'cooling off' period to reflect how to overcome the impasse[406] was agreed at the SPS Committee formal meeting in March 2015.

6.5.3 Outlook

Private standard-setting organisations will become legally relevant for WTO purposes, whereas they are considered a relevant international standard. In this context, it is argued here that an analogy to the relevant-standard test as introduced in the context of Article 2.4 of the TBT Agreement in US – Tuna II (Mexico) must be used to determine whether the SPS Agreement finds application for private food safety standards. In doing so, the legal playing field will be leveraged to the extent that all SPS measures, regardless of their public or private nature, will be covered by the SPS Agreement, thus acquiring a higher level of global legitimacy.

Although a further increase in the use of private food standards is feasible and not disputed here, national policy will determine the extent of their implications for international trade. It can therefore be predicted that, based on the level of domestic legislative activity, public standards will overlap and eventually marginalise the use of private food standards. This line of argumentation is further supported by the discussions carried out within the SPS Committee. In any event, public standards will

404 Committee on Sanitary and Phytosanitary Measures, March 2012, G/SPS/W/265; July 2012, G/SPS/W/265/Rev.1; 28 September 2012, G/SPS/W/265/Rev.2.

405 Committee on Sanitary and Phytosanitary Measures, Report of the Co-Stewards of the Private Standards E-Working Group on Action 1, 18 March 2014, G/SPS/W/276.

406 Committee on Sanitary and Phytosanitary Measures, Summary of the Meeting of 26–27 March 2015, Note by the Secretariat, 21 May 2015, G/SPS/R/78, p. 22.

still be necessary to correct market failures associated with information asymmetries or consumption externalities. They will therefore continue to play a key role in establishing a minimum level of protection to ensure the placing on the market of safe food as well as to prevent food fraud.

Much effort was put in bringing forward the agenda within the SPS Committee. Regrettably, the progress made to date has been minimal, particularly due to concerns raised by some developed countries that an agreement on a definition of SPS private standard could be potentially interpreted as falling within the scope of the SPS Agreement. It remains to be seen whether a private SPS measure will become the basis of a challenge before the WTO Dispute Settlement System. Until then, we are merely speculating. Ultimately, it can be argued that the decision to do business is an inherently private choice that may as well constitute an unintended effect of liberalised trade.

6.6 Conclusion

It remains undisputed that differing food safety standards arising from divergent regulatory approaches may impose important non-tariff barriers to trade in foodstuffs. The legal implications of food safety standards are far-reaching. Thus, this chapter has aimed at conceptualising the existing framework for sanitary and phytosanitary measures relevant to foodstuffs. In doing so, section II gave an overview of the historical inception of the SPS Agreement, the most important WTO instrument addressing food safety rules. It pointed out the delicate balance between liberalising markets and maintaining an appropriate national level of protection for the health and life of humans, animals and plants.

Section III examined the concept of SPS measures and identified four subcategories within the wide array of measures potentially falling within the scope of the SPS Agreement.

Section IV concentrated on the most relevant SPS principles for food standards. In doing so, it examined the role of international standards and harmonisation efforts, the obligation to base SPS measures on science and the rationale underlying the precautionary principle. The principle of mutual recognition or equivalence under the SPS Agreement was also addressed, partly laying down the basis for the two next chapters.

Finally, section V offered a case study on the widely-disputed use of private food safety standards. It addressed the possible legal status of such private SPS measures and the endevours undertaken by Members within the SPS Committee. Although five actions were agreed years ago, Members continue to struggle with the adoption of the first one. It remains to be seen whether the deadlock will be broken any time soon.

The next chapter turns the focus to regional regulatory approaches towards food standards. It will therefore examine the origin, development and implementation of the principle of mutual recognition in the European Union and its relevance for trade in food.

7. The Coordination of European Food Standards

7.1 Introduction

The impact attributed to WTO rules goes far beyond their implementation in national legislation. It also affects the way Members cooperate with one another on a bilateral level and their regional networks and agreements. NAFTA,[407] MERCOSUR,[408] ASEAN[409] and the EU offer some very concrete examples on the influence of international trade rules in their own regional organisations. Food standards play an important role in the international-regional dynamic. Depending on the regulatory approach preferred, coordination, harmonisation and equivalence will be more or less reflected in their own set of food trade rules.

In the EU, for instance, the impact attributed to its food legislation goes far beyond its mere application among its Member States. It expands across EU borders to influence the regulatory environment of third-party States. In fact, rules on the functioning of the EU Internal Market are looked upon with admiration, transposed onto foreign systems and sometimes even categorically rejected as means of keeping the power balance in international trade.[410] This is the reason underlying the following study on the EU coordination of non-harmonized areas of Food Law. Due to the less disputed nature of current harmonized areas of EU Food Law and based on the numerous amount of academic

407 North American Free Trade Agreement, 17 December 1992.

408 Mercado Común del Sur, *en.* Southern Common Market, 26 March 1991.

409 Association of Southeast Asian Nations, 28 January 1992.

410 See *e.g. EC – Hormones*; see *also*: WTO Joint Communication from the European Communities and the United States, EC-Measures concerning Meat and Meat Products (Hormones), 30 September 2009, WT/DS26/28.

attention it received,[411] this chapter will not address issues arising from them.[412] Food harmonisation examples in international trade law have been the subject matter of the previous chapters.[413] This chapter will instead examine the European non-harmonized areas of Food Law as an example of the implications of standard coordination in the emergence of new forms of global food governance.[414]

Section II will address the EU principles underlying the free movement of goods. In doing so, it will examine the three different regulatory approaches adopted in recent decades: the Old Approach, the New Approche and the Global Approach to EU regulation. Section III will analyse the importance of the ECJ jurisprudence in developing and advancing free trade in food. In particular, this section will examine the leading cases that contributed to the formation of the mutual recognition principles. Section IV will then describe the legislative change and solidification provoked by the rulings of the ECJ examined in the previous section. Section V will briefly conclude.

411 As recent as 2014, see: TOBIAS BAUMGARTNER/WESSELINA UEBE, European Union, in: EVELYN KIRCHSTEIGER-MEIER/TOBIAS BAUMGARTNER (eds), Global Food Legislation: An Overview, Wiley 2014, pp. 111–142; also *generally*: BERND VAN DER MEULEN/MENNO VAN DER VELDEN, European Food Law Handbook, Wageningen Academic Publishers 2008.

412 To name just a few, see *inter alia*: Reg. (EC) Nr. 1333/2008 of 16 December 2008 on Food Additives, OJ L 354/16; Reg. (EC) Nr. 396/2005 of 23 February 2005 on Maximum Residue Levels of Pesticides in or on Food and Feed of Plant and Animal Origin, OJ L 70/1; Reg. (EC) Nr. 852/2004 of 29 April 2004 on the Hygiene of Foodstuffs, OJ L 139/1; Reg. (EC) Nr. 853/2004 of 29 April 2004 on Hygiene for Food of Animal Origin, OJ L 226/22; Reg. (EC) Nr. 854/2004 of 29 April 2004 on Official Controls on Products of Animal Origin intended for Human Consumption, OJ L 226/83; EU Reg. Nr. 1169/2011 of 25 October 2011 on the Provision of Food Information to Consumers, OJ L 304/18; Reg. (EC) Nr. 1829/2003 of 22 September 2003 on Genetically Modified Food and Feed, OJ L 268/1.

413 Notably under WTO law through the SPS, TBT and TRIPS Agreement.

414 This Chapter is partly based on a previously published article: MARIELA MAIDANA-ELETTI, Trade in Foodstuffs: The Impact of EU Internal Market Rules on Swiss Food Legislation, in: MARIELA MAIDANA-ELETTI/CARLY TOEPKE, Recht und Gesellschaft, Schulthess 2014, pp. 141–166.

7.2 EU Principles on the Free Movement of Goods

The coordination of the European food market has been a priority for the European legislators since the foundation of the European Communities.[415] Therefore, the principles governing intra-communitary trade constitute an essential instrument in ensuring the correct functioning of the common market.[416] The umbrella provisions are found in the Treaty on the Functioning of the European Union (TFEU).[417] In particular, Article 26.1 TFEU establishes that:

> [T]he Union shall adopt measures with the aim of establishing or ensuring the functioning of the internal market [...].[418]

The TFEU further delimits its sphere of application by stating that the internal market comprises an area without frontiers in which the free movement of goods is ensured.[419] Consequently, free trade as established in Article 28 TFEU[420] is composed by a customs union which prohibits both the imposition of custom duties and quantitative restrictions on imports

415 PAUL CRAIG/GRAINNE DE BÚRCA, EU Law – Text, Cases and Materials, 5th ed., Oxford University Press, 2011, p. 594 *et seq.*; SEBASTIAN KRAPOHL, 'Thalidomide, BSE, and the Single Market: An Historical-Institutionalist Approach to Regulatory Regimes in the European Union', (2007) 46 European Journal of Political Research, pp. 25–46, p. 38.

416 ALEMANNO, p. 34; TOBIAS BAUMGARTNER, Allgemeiner Regelungsrahmen im EU-Lebensmittelrecht, in: ROLF WEBER/URS KLEMM/TOBIAS BAUMGARTNER/NINA GROLIMUND/DIRK TRÜTEN, Lebensmittelrecht EU-Schweiz, 2nd ed., Schulthess 2006, pp. 53–76, p. 71 [BAUMGARTNER], RUDOLF STREINZ, Europarecht, 6th ed., C.F. Müller 2003, p. 306. On the functioning of the internal market in general *see*: DAMIAN CHALMERS/GARETH DAVIES/GIORGIO MONTI, European Union Law: Cases and Materials, 2nd ed., Cambridge University Press 2010, pp. 675–686 [CHALMERS *et al.*].

417 EUROPEAN PARLIAMENT, Treaty on the Functioning of the European Union, 9 May 2008, OJ C 115/47 [TFEU].

418 Art. 26.1 of the TFEU.

419 Art. 26.2 of the TFEU.

420 Art. 28.1 of the TFEU states that: 'The Union shall comprise a customs union which shall cover all trade in goods and which shall involve the prohibition between Member States of customs duties on imports and exports and of all charges having equivalent effect [...].'

and exports as well as those measures having an equivalent effect between EU Member States.[421]

The exception to this rule can be found in Article 36 TFEU, which establishes that:

> The provisions of Articles 34 and 35 shall not preclude prohibitions or restrictions on imports, exports or goods in transit justified on grounds of public morality, public policy or public security; the protection of health and life of humans, animals or plants [...]. Such prohibitions or restrictions shall not, however, constitute a means of arbitrary discrimination or a disguised restriction on trade between Member States.

The divergence in food safety laws among Member States and the likelihood of national trade-restrictive measures to fall within the scope of Article 36 TFEU triggered the proliferation of EU horizontal regulation for foodstuffs as a means of removing these trade barriers.[422] The harmonisation of national legislation would then ensure equivalence between imported and domestically produced goods.

7.2.1 The Old Approach

The European Commission launched the now-called Old Approach to legislative harmonisation in its 1969 General Program for the elimination of technical barriers to trade.[423] The obstacles to the free movement of foodstuffs posed by diverging domestic measures was identified as a priority. As such, the EC set up 43 key areas that needed harmonised legislation, divided into five different phases.[424] The drafting of mainly recipe legislation, in areas that are predominantly vertical, translated into obligatory designations for food products with clearly defined compositions. The painstaking work involved in this program meant that

421 Art. 30 of the TFEU in conjunction with Art. 34 and Art. 35 of the TFEU.

422 ALEMANNO, p. 43; RICHARD WALLIS, Guide to European Law and Institutions, Straightforward Publishing 2007, p. 62.

423 EUROPEAN COMMISSION, General Program for the Elimination of the Technical Barriers to Trade, adopted by the European Council in its Resolution [1969], OJ C-76/1 [EC General Program].

424 Including, among others, sugar, butter, cacao, soft drinks, cheese and beer.

designated deadlines could not be kept. In 1973, the European Council adopted the Industrial Policy Program with the aim of adopting 35 directives on the compositional standards for foodstuffs.[425] These directives designed standards for permissible ingredients in order to facilitate intra-community trade.[426] The Old Approach to harmonisation failed to achieve the goals it was designed for.[427] Sixteen years after its launch, the old approach facilitated the adoption of only a third out of all the priority areas.[428] The European Commission needed a new strategy.

7.2.2 The New Approach

In order to overcome the limitations posed by the old approach, the European Commission launched the New Approach to harmonisation and national legislation in 1985.[429] It based the foundations on the principles developed years earlier by the ECJ, particularly the mutual recognition principle.

According to the New Approach, positive integration aiming at harmonising national rules would be adopted where there was a need to protect public health and consumer interests, to ensure fair trade and to provide appropriate official controls.[430] The rationale behind this approach was to lay down horizontal, harmonised rules establishing the

425 EUROPEAN COUNCIL, Resolution on Industrial Policy, 17 December 1973, OJ C 117.

426 See *e.g.* sugar, honey, coffee extracts and chicory extracts, fruit jams, jellies and marmalades.

427 PAUL GREY, Food Law and the Internal Market: Taking Stock, (1990) 15 (2) Food Policy, p. 112.

428 EUROPEAN COMMISSION, Community Legislation on Foodstuffs, 8 November 1985, COM(85)603 final, p. 3 [EC Community Legislation on Foodstuffs].

429 EUROPEAN COMMISSION, White Paper on Completing the Single Market, COM(85)310 final, 14 June 1985; EUROPEAN COMMISSION, Green Paper on the Development of Standardisation: Action for Faster Techincal Integration in Europe, COM(90)456 final, 8 October 1990.

430 See *generally*: JACQUES PELKMANS, 'The New Approach to Technical Harmonization and Standardization' (1987) 25 Journal of Common Market Studies, pp. 249–269; ANDREW MCGEE/STEPHEN WEATHERHILL, 'The Evolution of the Single Market: Harmonisation or Liberalisation?' (1990) 53 The Modern Law Review, pp. 578–596.

minimum standard of legality (essential requirements) and to delegate the details to standards organisations, which would in turn be coordinated by national conformity assessment bodies.[431] The directives adopted during this phase contained positive lists that dealt with the essential requirements of EU law.[432]

It must be noted here that the main aim of European food legislation up to this point remained the removal of barriers to trade.[433] The protection of public health through food safety measures remained a secondary effect of the pathway to free trade.[434] It was only after the BSE crisis[435] that the ECJ shifted its case law to give precedence to the protection of public health over economic considerations.[436]

431 This line of argumentation is also found in GREGORY SHAFFER, 'Reconciling Trade and Regulatory Goals: The Prospects and Limits of New Approaches to Transatlantic Governance Through the Mutual Recognition and Safe Harbour Agreements' (2002) 9 Columbia Journal of European Law, pp. 29–77, p. 33.

432 Among others, additives, extraction solvents, flavouring agents, colours, sweeteners, food additives other than colours and sweeteners, labelling foods for particular nutritional needs, hygiene and official controls.

433 EUROPEAN COMMISSION, Enhancing the Implementation of New Approach Directives, COM(2003)240, 7 May 2003 (not published in the OJ).

434 *Cf.* ELLEN VOS, 'EU Food Safety Regulation in the Aftermath of the BSE Crisis' (2000) 23 Journal of Consumer Policy, pp. 227–255, p. 233.

435 For a legal analysis on the impact of the BSE crisis on European food legislation see: ALBERTO ALEMANNO, Food Safety and the Single European Market, in: DAVID VOGEL/CHRISTOPH ANSELL, What's the Beef? The Contested Governance of European Food Safety, MIT Press 2006, pp. 237–358; MORITZ HAGENMEYER, 'Modern Food Safety Requirements – According to EC Regulation 178/2002' (2002) 4 Zeitschrift für das gesamte Lebensmittelrecht, pp. 443–459; SEBASTIAN KRAPOHL, 'Risk Regulation in the EU between interests and expertise – The Case of BSE' (2003) 10 Journal of European Public Policy, pp. 189–207; KEITH VINCENT, 'Mad Cows and Eurocrats – Community Responses to the BSE Crisis' (2004) 10 (5) European Law Journal, pp. 499–517; MICHELLE EVERSON/ELLEN VOS (eds), The Scientification of Politics and the Politisation of Science, Uncertain Risks Regulated, Routledge-Cavendish 2009, p. 1–2.

436 Affish BV v. Rijksdienst voor de Keuring van Vee en Vlees [1997], Judgment of 17 July 1997, Case C-183/95, ECR 4315, para. 43.

7.2.2.1 The EU Green Paper on Food Safety

The European Community published the Green Paper on Food Safety in 1997 with the aim of encouraging public debate on the best ways to regulate food.[437] It advocated for the need for a European policy that focuses on safe food in order to protect consumers and their health.[438] To achieve these objectives, the Commission proposed to adopt a scientific approach when adopting new legislative measures or the precautionary principle in cases where scientific evidence was lacking or incomplete. It also proposed to design control and inspection measures to be taken along the food supply chain, to inform consumers about the nature and content of the food as well as to establish clear responsibilities for the controlling agents.[439]

In fact, the Commission aimed at communicating that the role of the Community was not to replace the official controls carried out by Member States. Rather, its objective was to verify that the necessary official controls were being carried out throughout the EU in the first place.[440]

7.2.2.2 The EC Communication on Consumer Health and Safety

Shortly after the publication of the White Paper on Food Safety, the European Commission published a communication on consumer health and safety to set out the actions taken to use scientific evidence and manage official controls.[441]

This approach was based on the doctrine of risk analysis and a separation between risk management (the process of weighing policy alternatives based on the results of risk assessments),[442] risk assessment (the science-based process that identifies and characterises hazards),[443]

437 European Commission, Green Paper on the General Principles of Food Law in the European Union, 30 April 1997, COM(97)176 [Green Paper on Food Safety].

438 Green Paper on Food Safety, p. 3.

439 Green Paper on Food Safety, para. 11–12.

440 Alemanno, p. 64.

441 European Commission, Communication on Consumer Health and Food Safety, COM(97)183 final, 30 April 1997 [EC Communication on Consumer Health and Food Safety].

442 Definition given by the Codex Alimentarius.

443 Definition given by the Codex Alimentarius.

risk management and control inspections and transparency.[444] With the adoption of the risk analysis doctrine, the foundations for a new EU food policy regime were laid.

7.2.2.3 The EU White Paper on Food Safety

In 2000, the European Commission contributed to speeding up the process of EU food policy reform by proposing an institutional reform based on the need for major structural change.[445] To achieve this, the Commission proposed the creation of a European food authority that could guarantee safe food. The hypothesis was that a comprehensive and integrated approach to food safety would inevitably lead to a more effective food policy.[446]

In particular, the White Paper on Food Safety called for establishing a European Food Safety Authority entrusted with risk assessment and risk communication (but not risk management), and for adopting new legislation laying down the general principles of food law, while consistently implementing a 'farm to the table' approach through the adoption of 84 different measures. It also re-established the Rapid Alert System[447] as a key instrument on coordinating the exchange of information between the Commission and Member States by imposing on economic operators the obligation to announce food safety emergencies.

7.2.3 The Global Approach

Eventually, Reg. (EC) Nr. 178/2002 was adopted to horizontally harmonise all stages of production, as well as the processing and distribution of food and feed.[448] This regulation aimed at achieving a high level of

444 EC Communication on Consumer Health and Food Safety, p. 9–10.

445 European Commission, White Paper on Food Safety, COM(99)719, 12 January 2000 (unspecified) [White Paper on Food Safety].

446 Alemanno, p. 69.

447 The Rapid Alert System for Foodstuffs (RASFF) was established by the Council Directive 92/59/EEC on General Product Safety, 19 June 1992, OJ L 228/24.

448 European Parliament, Reg. (EC) Nr. 178/2002 of 28 January 2002 on the General Principles and Requirements of Food Law, establishing the European Food Safety Authority and laying down Procedures in matters of Food Safety, OJ L 31/1 [Reg. (EC) 178/2002].

protection of human health and consumer interests, as well as ensuring the functioning of the internal market by establishing a comprehensive EU food policy regime and by creating the European Food Safety Authority.[449] The adoption of Reg. (EC) Nr. 178/2002 sets a clear example of positive integration rules aiming at the horizontal harmonisation in a specific area such as Food Law. Since its adoption, it has succeeded in removing trade barriers by establishing equal public mandatory food safety requirements between Member States.

Despite the success with the horizontal harmonisation of European Food Law, many areas affecting trade in foodstuffs remain divergent. The legal uncertainty created by the (in)application of varied national legislation raises concerns about its compatibility with the EU principles of intra-communitary trade. For decades now, the European Court of Justice has been successfully dealing with issues arising from non-harmonised areas of (food) law and its influence on the correct functioning of the internal market.

7.3 The Importance of ECJ Jurisprudence for EU Food Law

Trade barriers can be removed through a decision taken by a Member State, but also through a ruling of the European Court of Justice (ECJ) about the incompatibility of a national provision with the TFEU.[450] The ECJ has rendered numerous cases on national non-compliant rules on trade in foodstuffs. The leading cases are briefly described in the following section.

449 Examining the origins of the European Food Safety Authority (EFSA) *see*: ALEMANNO, p. 72.

450 YOUNG ALASDAIR, The Politics of Regulation and the Internal Market, in: KNUD JORGENSEN/MARK POLLACK/BEN ROSAMOND, Handbook of European Union Politics, Sage Publications Ltd. 2007, pp. 373–394, p. 378.

7.3.1 Dassonville and Trade-Restrictive Measures

Dassonville[451] dealt with parallel imports of Scottish whisky into Belgium, where a certificate of origin was required for all whisky sold within its national territory. Unable to obtain British certificates of origin in France for re-importation into Belgium, Mr. Dassonville was accused of fraud and criminally prosecuted. A question about the legality of Belgian laws requiring an official document issued by the government of the exporting country for products bearing a designation of origin was submitted to the ECJ. The court ruled that the Belgian legislation was trade-restrictive and amounted to a measure having an equivalent effect to a quantitative restriction. Furthermore, the ECJ held that every measure indirectly or potentially affecting the intra-communitary flow of goods between States in a negative manner is in principle prohibited under Article 34 TFEU.[452] The broad margin of application created by this judgment, which extended to virtually all non-harmonised domestic legislation in every area, was soon to be restricted by the findings in Cassis de Dijon.

7.3.2 Cassis de Dijon and the Origins of Equivalence

The facts of this case referred to a German measure prohibiting the distribution of liquor with less than 25% alcohol. Based on this measure, a French type of liquor – crème de Cassis – which contained less than the minimum quantity of alcohol according to German legislation, was prohibited from entering the German market. The German national court called upon to solve this dispute decided to refer the question of compatibility with EU law to the ECJ.

The ECJ concluded that products which have been lawfully produced and marketed in one of the Member States may not be kept out of the market of another Member State on grounds of non-compliance with

451 Procureur du Roi v. Benoit and Gustave Dassonville [1974] Case C-8/74, Judgment of 11 July 1974, ECR 837 [Dassonville].

452 Dassonville, paras. 6–9.

national law.[453] This followed as a result of the ECJ's interpretation of the notion of measures as having an equivalent effect to the quantitative restrictions pursuant to Art. 34 TFEU. Hence, the principle of mutual recognition came into existence: products are deemed to be legally marketed as long as they comply with the national technical requirements of any given Member State.

Conversely, consumer protection no longer provides legitimate grounds for prohibiting the marketing of foodstuffs that are different in composition to the products usually sold in the territory of any given Member State.[454] The legitimate aim of protecting consumers may now be achieved by less trade-restrictive means, such as the inclusion of additional information on product labels to allow more informed choices.[455] In particular, the precedent set by Cassis de Dijon demonstrates that, in order to guarantee the free movement of goods, the application of the mutual recognition principle often functions as a legislative waiver to harmonise mandatory food requirements.[456] As such, Member States are allowed to maintain their own quality and technical standards so long as they do not have a trade-restrictive effect on the internal market.[457] The ECJ so chose country of origin regulation.[458]

453 Rewe-Zentral AG v. Bundesmonopolverwaltung für Branntwein [1978] Case C-120/78, Judgement of 20 February 1979, ECR 649 [Cassis de Dijon].

454 Cassis de Dijon, para. 13–14; Chalmers *et al.*, p. 697; Catherine Barnard, The Substantive Law of the EU, 4th ed., Oxford University Press 2013, p. 94; Susan Schmidt, 'Mutual Recognition as a New Mode of Governance' (2007) 14(5) Journal of European Public Policy, pp. 367–381.

455 Chalmers *et al.*, p. 697, Alemanno, p. 55; Baumgarter, p. 73.

456 *Cf.* Alemanno, pp. 41–42.

457 *Cf.* European Communities v. Federal Republic of Germany (Reinheitsgebot) [1987], Case C-178/84, Judgment of 12 May 1987, ECR 1227, para. 35, where the ECJ recognised as legitimate for a Member State to give its consumers the necessary information which will enable them to make choices based on that consideration.

458 Also described as 'principle of tolerance'; *see*: Gareth Davies, Is Mutual Recognition an Alternative to Harmonisation: Lessons on Trade and Tolerance of Diversity from the EU, in: Federico Ortino/Lorand Bartels (eds), Regional Trade Agreements and the WTO, Oxford University Press 2006, pp. 265–280.

7.3.3 Keck and Selling Arrangements

This is the last of three landmark cases that define the scope of Article 34 TFEU.[459] Bernhard Keck and Daniel Mithouart were being prosecuted in France for having resold products at a lower than the actual purchase price. French legislation prohibited resale at a loss. The French courts decided to refer a compatibility question to the ECJ.

After due consideration, the ECJ held that certain selling agreements do not fall within the scope of Article 34 TFEU, as long as they affect the marketing of domestic products in the same manner as those products from another Member State.[460] While excluding all applicable selling arrangements, the scope of application of Article 34 TFEU has been considerably reduced.

7.4 The Development of the Mutual Recognition Principle

7.4.1 Limiting the Scope of Application

Given the broad definition of 'trade barriers' given by the ECJ,[461] the European Commission considered it necessary to narrow the scope of interpretation in order to monitor more strictly the application of rules on the free movement of goods.[462]

The EC Communication on Cassis de Dijon[463] emphasized the need to justify the precedence of technical rules aiming at the protection of

459 Bernhard Keck and Daniel Mithouard [1993] Joined Cases C-267/91 and C-268/91, Judgement of 24 November 1993, ECR I 6097 [Keck].

460 Keck, para. 16–17.

461 Cassis de Dijon, stating: 'Any national measure capable of hindering, directly or indirectly, actually or potentially, intra-communitary trade'.

462 *Cf.* Laurence Gormley, 'Cassis de Dijon and the Communication from the Commission' (1981) 6 European Law Review, pp. 454–459.

463 European Commission, Communication concerning the Consequences of the Judgment given by the Court of Justice on 20 February 1979 in Case 120/78 (Cassis de Dijon), OJ C 256/2, 3 October 1980 [EC Communication on Cassis de Dijon].

essential general interests over fundamental rules of EU Law.[464] More importantly, the European Commission stated that the proper functioning of the internal market could only be guaranteed where Member States give due consideration to the legitimate requirements of other Member States while drafting their own technical rules.[465] These legitimate requirements constitute mandatory requirements, if they are justified on exception grounds – such as the protection of public health – and are proportionate to the objective of that particular measure.[466]

As a result of this strict criteria, a whole body of commercial rules, and in particular those referring to the composition, designation, presentation and packaging of products, was addressed in the Communication to ensure coherence within the European system.[467] However, concerns were raised about the active quasi-judicial role played by the European Commission with this Communication, particularly due to the political aspects of its policy statement.[468]

7.4.2 Improving Effectiveness

Although the principle of mutual recognition has been producing tangible results in ensuring the free movement of goods during recent decades, concerns have been raised by Members States and economic operators about its effective application.

The European Commission, as requested by the European Council and the European Parliament,[469] proposed in a further Communication a

464 EC Communication on Cassis de Dijon, p. 1.

465 EC Communication on Cassis de Dijon, p. 1.

466 Frans-Nederlandse Maatschappij Voor Biologische Producten [1981], Case C 272/80, Judgement of 17 December 1981, ECR 3277, para. 12; Sandoz [1983], Case-C 174/82, Judgement of 14 July 1983, ECR 2445, para. 18.

467 EC Communication on Cassis de Dijon, p. 1.

468 Michelle Egan, Constructing a European Market, Oxford University Press 2001, p. 109; Nicholas Bernard, On the Art of Not Mixing One's Drinks: Dassonville and Cassis de Dijon Revisited, in: Miguel Maduro/Loic Azoulai (eds), The Past and Future of EU Law, Hart Publishing 2001, pp. 456–464 at p. 457.

469 European Council, 2094th Council Meeting on the Internal Market, Press Release, 18 May 1998, available at <http://europa.eu/rapid/press-release_PRES-98-148_en.htm> (last visited: 30 June 2015).

series of initiatives to improve the implementation of mutual recognition as a crucial tool in ensuring the observance of national traditions and in maintaining a diversity of products on the internal market.[470] It was concluded that the lack of knowledge about the ways the principle functions, together with the lack of knowledge about the extent of its implications on the part of both the competent authorities and the economic operators, constituted the main obstacle for more efficient results.[471]

To tackle these issues, the Commission, proposed several measures to enhance the credibility of monitoring systems and to improve the information flow of the players involved.[472] It comes as no surprise that the food sector ranked first on the list of most commonly affected sectors by infringements of the mutual recognition principle.[473] It was only a few months later when the Council welcomed the Commission's Communication, calling for a simplification of relevant national legislation and its application procedures.[474]

7.4.3 EU Harmonization of Technical Rules

It was not until the adoption of Reg. (EC) No 764/2008[475] that obstacles to the correct application of the principle of mutual recognition, such as lack of awareness, complex administrative procedures and insufficient information about different national legislations were addressed in a uniform manner.

In particular, this regulation makes reference to the application of technical rules by means of mandatory prior authorisation procedures

470 European Commission, Communication on the Mutual Recognition in the Context of the Follow-up to the Action Plan for the Single Market, COM(1999)299 final, 16 June 1999 [EC Communication on Mutual Recognition of the Follow-up].

471 EC Communication on Mutual Recognition of the Follow-up, p. 1.

472 EC Communication on Mutual Recognition of the Follow-up, pp. 7–12.

473 EC Communication on Mutual Recognition of the Follow-up, p. 13.

474 European Council, Resolution of 28 October 1999 on Mutual Recognition, 19 May 2000, OJ C 141, pp. 5–6.

475 European Parliament, Reg. (EC) Nr. 764/2008 of 9 July 2008 on the Procedures relating to the Application of Certain National Technical Rules to Products lawfully marketed in another Member State, OJ L 218/21 [Reg. (EC) Nr. 764/2008].

(positive list). Although national competent authorities may restrict the free movement of goods by rejecting an application to place a certain product on the market, the procedure applied ought to respond to a public-interest objective that complies with EU law, as well as being proportionate and non-discriminatory.[476] In other words, Reg. (EC) 764/2008 provides national competent authorities with a procedure that allows more effective communication with economic operators.[477]

As a result, the imposition of national technical requirements will be incompatible with EU Law unless it can be proved that overriding reasons of public interest and a lack of less trade-restrictive measures justify their application.[478] Furthermore, the scope of application of Reg. (EC) Nr. 764/2008 includes administrative decisions in the form of technical rules that may hinder the placement of a product on the market lawfully marketed in another Member State.[479]

In particular, Reg. (EC) Nr. 764/2008 finds application in cases where a national competent authority intends to adopt a measure that:

a) is an administrative decision;
b) concerns a product lawfully marketed in another Member State;
c) concerns a product that is not subject to harmonised EU law;
d) is addressed to an economic operator;
e) is based on a technical rule; and

476 Reg. (EC) Nr. 764/2008, p. 22.

477 Reg. (EC) Nr. 764/2008, p. 24.

478 The concept of overriding reasons of public interest has been constantly developed by the ECJ through Case Law; see, among others: Ker Optika bt v. ANTSZ Del-dunanruli Regionalis Intezete [2010] Case C-108/09, Judgment of 25 November 2010, ECR I 1039, para. 57 [Ker Optika]; Commission of the European Communities v. Portugal [2010] Case C-458/08, Judgment of 18 November 2010, ECR I 11599; Commission of the European Communities v. Italian Republic [2009] Case C-110/05, Judgment of 10 February 2009, ECR I 519, para. 33; Commission of the European Communities v. Federal Republic of Germany [2007] Case C-490/04, Judgment of 18 July 2007, ECR I 6095; Commission of the European Communities v. Kingdom of Belgium [2006] Case C-433/04, Judgment of 9 November 2006, ECR I 10653.

479 Art. 2 of Reg. (EC) Nr. 764/2008.

f) its direct or indirect effects lead to a prohibition on the placing on the market of that product, modification or additional testing of that product before being placed on the market or withdrawal from the market.[480]

More importantly, Reg. (EC) Nr. 764/2008 establishes product contact points to ensure the flow of communication between competent authorities and business operators.[481] Reg. (EC) Nr. 764/2008 also introduced the *written notice* requirement, under which failure to notify the economic operator of a decision based on technical rules (such as food recipe laws, namely public mandatory standards) within the specified period, renders a product as lawfully marketed in the concerned Member State.[482]

7.4.4 Defining EU Technical Rules

The European Commission also published a guidance document on the application of Reg. (EC) Nr. 764/2008 to food supplements.[483] It defines the concept of technical rule as:

> Any provision of law, regulation or other administrative decision of a Member State which (a) is not subject to harmonized EU law; (b) prohibits in its territory the marketing of food supplements lawfully marketed in another Member State [...] and (c) lays down the characteristics required of that (type of) food supplement such as levels of quality, performance or safety [...].[484]

It is of interest to recall in this context that the ECJ recognised consumer protection as a legitimate aim constituting an overriding reason

480 Art. 2 of Reg. (EC) Nr. 764/2008.
481 Art. 9 to 11 of Reg. (EC) Nr. 764/2008.
482 Art. 6 of Reg. (EC) Nr. 764/2008.
483 European Commission, Guidance Document on the Application of the Mutual Recognition Regulation (EC) 764/2008 to Food Supplements, 1 February 2010, available at: <http://ec.europa.eu/enterprise/policies/single-market-goods/files/mutual-recognition/food-supplements/food-supplements_en.pdf> (last visited: 30 June 2015) [EC Guidance Document].
484 EC Guidance Document, para. 4.4.1.

of public interest to allow the application of national technical rules.[485] Accordingly, national legislation encompassing technical requirements has to fulfill two requirements in order not to fall within the scope of Article 34 TFEU. First, the measures in question must apply to all relevant traders operating within a given national territory. Second, the measure must affect in the same manner, in law and in fact, the selling of domestic products and the selling of those from other Member States.[486]

In cases where national technical requirements constitute a measure having an effect equivalent to a quantitative restriction as prohibited by Article 34 TFEU, the restriction on the free movement of goods must be objectively justified on one of the overriding reasons of public interest set out in Article 36 TFEU. The ECJ held in this regard that the legislation in question must be appropriate and necessary, bearing in mind the measure of discretion allocated to Member States to determine the level of protection of public health and the way in which that level may be achieved.[487]

7.5 Conclusion

Although the establishment of recipe food laws is no longer a priority for the EU,[488] the need for mandatory quality standards remains essential in order to determine whether a product can be placed on a particular market.[489] After the entering into force of Reg. (EC) Nr. 764/2008, and in the light of ECJ Case Law, however, the costs of maintaining and

485 Commission of the European Communities v. Italian Republic [2007] Case C- 260/04, Judgement of 13 September 2007, ECR I 708, para. 27; Massimiliano Placanica and Others [2007] Cases C-338/04, C-359/04 and C-360/04, Judgement of 6 March 2007, ECR I-1891, para. 45.

486 Ker-Optika, para. 52.

487 Ker-Optika, para. 58; Jose Manuel Blanco Perez and Maria del Pilar Chao Gomez [2010] Joined Cases C-570/07 and C-571/07, Judgement of 1 June 2010, ECR I 4629, para. 44.

488 The new approach to food law after 1985 meant that priority was given to consumer protection and fair-trade instead of focusing on quality legislation. See ALEMANNO, p. 59; O'ROURKE, p. 101.

489 O'ROURKE, p. 101.

enforcing national quality standards in non-harmonised areas of Food Law have increased. Conversely, technical rules on the composition of foodstuffs will be subject to deeper legal scrutiny each time the competent authority of a Member State renders an administrative decision regarding a product lawfully marketed in another Member State.

This chapter has addressed the European regulatory framework for foodstuffs. EU principles underlying the free movement of goods were the object of study in section II, where the different regulatory approaches applied in recent decades were identified and analysed. From the old to the new and global approach, the legislative history of European Food Law is a rich one. Section III continued with an analysis of leading ECJ Case Law. Dasonville, Cassis de Dijon and Keck laid the foundation for the creation of one of the pillars of EU Internal Market Law: the principle of mutual recognition. Its legislative solidification was the focus of section IV. The development of the mutual recognition principle has undoubtedly promoted free movement of goods, while at the same time gradually dismantling trade barriers between Member States. This deduction has been made throughout this chapter while examining the European regulatory system applicable to trade. It concluded that the mutual recognition principle is the most efficient available means of ensuring the free movement of foodstuffs subject to non-harmonised rules within the EU.

As the legal principles laid out in the analysed WTO instruments influence regional legislation, so does regional legislation influence domestic orders. The next and final chapter will therefore turn to examining the implications of European Food Law in Swiss legislation governing the trade in foodstuffs.

8. The Equivalence of Swiss Food Standards

8.1 Introduction

In spite of its geographical situation, Switzerland has remained outside the European adherence process. It sits at the heart of the European continent, yet it has decided to remain politically and economically detached from the EU. However, recently enacted laws and regulations, as a reflection of their social and economic status, have been increasingly adapted to those of the main trading partners worldwide. This tendency has also been observed in Switzerland.[490]

The Swiss and European legal framework for foodstuffs provides a good example of coordination and equivalence regulatory approaches. For example, until recently, for a foreign product to be placed on the Swiss market, it had to comply with a series of public mandatory quality standards that were established at the ordinance level. This situation changed radically once the unilateral adoption of the Cassis-de-Dijon Principle entered into forced in 2011. According to the new legislation, a Swiss manufacturer may choose to produce for the domestic market according to EU technical quality requirements if doing so proves to be economically more beneficial than compliance with costly Swiss quality standards. Although still in force, Swiss public mandatory standards have become *de facto* non-mandatory law.

This chapter builds on the previous one. It aims at illustrating regulatory equivalence within new forms of food governance. In doing so, it

490 For a comprehensive political analysis of the theory of autonomous implementation and its applicability in Switzerland *see*: ROY GAVA/FREDERIC VARONE, So Close, Yet so Far? The EU's Footprint in Swiss Legislative Legislation, in: SYLVAIN BROUARD/OLIVIER COSTA/THOMAS KÖNIG (eds), The Europeanization of Domestic Legislation: The Empirical Implications of the Delors' Myth in Nine Countries, Springer 2012, pp. 197–221; ANDREAS KELLERHALS/TOBIAS BAUMGARTNER, 'Das Cassis-de-Dijon-Prinzip und die Schweiz' (2006) 102 Schweizerische Juristenzeitung, pp. 321–330.

analyses the trade-related implications of food equivalence. It does not, however, deal with administrative or procedural aspects of the unilateral introduction of the mutual recognition principle in Switzerland, such as the placing in the market of foodstuffs subject to a permit or the standing to lodge a complaint (so-called 'Klagelegitimation') before Swiss courts.

Section II lays out the applicable legal framework to trade in foodstuffs between Switzerland and the EU. In particular, this section examines the various concluded free trade agreements. Section III addresses the Swiss legal framework applicable to trade in food after the recent legislative developments adopting the European principle of mutual recognition. Section IV summarises the findings of this chapter and briefly concludes.

8.2 The Legal Framework for Trade Relations between the EU and Switzerland

Switzerland exports nearly two-thirds of its products to the EU. Switzerland is also the third most important market for EU products after the USA and Russia.[491] Along with the other members of the European Free Trade Association (EFTA),[492] Switzerland negotiated the creation of the European Economic Area (EEA)[493] based on four fundamental freedoms:

491 Swiss Confederation, Federal Department of Foreign Affairs (FDFA), Bilateral Agreements Switzerland-EU, 17 August 2009, available at: <http://www.europa.admin.ch/index.html?lang=en> (last visited: 30 June 2015) [FDFA Bilateral Agreements Switzerland-EU].

492 Norway, Lichtenstein, Iceland; *see*: Agreement on the Creation of the European Free Trade Association (EFTA), 4 January 1960, SR 0.632.31.

493 Dirk Trüten, Einfluss des EG-Lebensmittelrechts auf das schweizerische Recht, in: Rolf Weber/Urs Klemm/Tobias Baumgartner/Nina Grolimund/Dirk Trüten, Lebensmittelrecht EG-Schweiz, Schulthess 2006, p. 105; Roger Zäch, Gesamtüberblick, in: Daniel Thürer/Rolf Weber/Roger Zäch, Bilaterale Verträge EG-Schweiz: Ein Handbuch, Schultess 2002, p. 4 [Zäch]; Swiss Confederation, Federal Department of Foreign Affairs (FDFA), Bilateral Agreements Switzerland-EU: Fact Sheets, 2 November 2007, p. 6; available at: <www.bundespublikationen.admin.ch> (last visited: 30 June 2015) [FDFA Bilateral Agreements Switzerland-EU: Fact Sheets].

the movement of people, goods, capital and services. At the same time, Switzerland even submitted a request to begin negotiations for membership in the European Community.

However, after the rejection through referendum by the Swiss people in December 1992, the Swiss Federal Council decided instead to follow the so-called 'bilateral path' with the EU. As a result, Switzerland has been continuously looking for compatible legal solutions to remove major trade barriers with its main trading partner.[494]

In order to create the best possible legal framework for economic relations between Switzerland and the EU, several instruments have been developed: the so-called autonomous implementation of European legislation for one, as well as the signing of agreements such as the Free Trade Agreement (FTA), the Bilateral I and the Bilateral II, all of which are based on a classic form of cooperation between governments that excludes the transfer of powers to a supranational body.[495]

8.2.1 The 1972 Free Trade Agreement (FTA)

The 1972 FTA[496] between Switzerland and the EU was one of enormous economic importance, and thus it is regarded as one of the main pillars for their trade relations. It created a free trade zone for industrial products originating in Switzerland[497] and in the States Parties to the

494 See *generally*: ANDREAS KELLERHALS/TOBIAS BAUMGARTNER, A Different Neighborhood Policy: Switzerland's Approach to European Integration, Schulthess 2014; THOMAS COTTIER/MATTHIAS OESCH, International Trade Regulation: Law and Policy in the WTO, the European Union and Switzerland, Cases, Materials and Comments, Cameron May 2005; FRITZ BREUSS/THOMAS COTTIER/PETER-CHRISTIAN MÜLLER-GRAFF (eds), Die Schweiz im europäischen Integrationsprozess, Helbing Lichtenhahn 2008.

495 ZÄCH, p. 8.

496 Agreement between the Swiss Confederation and the European Economic Comminities, 22 July 1972, SR 0.632.401.

497 Such as watches or machines, which are of major importance for the Swiss economy.

FTA. It prohibits the imposition of quotas, tariffs and measures that would have an equivalent effect in the sense of Article 36 TFEU.[498]

The 1972 FTA does not apply to agricultural products, with the exception of processed agricultural products (such as chocolate and pasta), which enjoy special status.[499]

Unlike a customs union, free trade partners determine their own external customs tariffs and quotas independently. Hence, customs clearance still takes place at borders between partners to ensure the application of the FTA to products originating in one of the contracting parties.[500] This resulted in a progressive abolition of custom duties between Switzerland and the EU.

8.2.2 Bilateral Agreements

In 1993, Switzerland initiated negotiations in seven sectors with the EU in order to pursue their relations on a bilateral basis. The EU, however, set two main conditions for the negotiations. First, all the agreements had to be negotiated at the same time, and second, all the agreement had to be signed and take effect together.

This parallelism, also called a 'link-up clause', originated in the belief that negotiations would lead to a win-win situation only if the different agreements were adopted as a package.[501] These agreements were linked by a 'guillotine clause', which established that, in case of

498 *Cf.* THOMAS COTTIER/MATTHIAS OEASCH, 'Switzerland' in: GEORGE ANDERSON (ed), Internal Markets and Multi-Level Governance, Oxford University Press 2012, pp. 131–159, p. 133; RUDOLF STREINZ, Die Europäisierung des Lebensmittelrechts, in: THOMAS POLEDNA/OLIVIER ARTER/MONIKA GATTIKER, Lebensmittelrecht, Stämpfli 2006, p. 200.

499 These products are both industrial and agricultural. Therefore, they have been regulated in Protocol II FTA, which was later modified by the Agreement between the EC and the Swiss Confederation amending the Agreement between the European Economic Community and the Swiss Confederation of 22 July 1972 as regards the provision applicable to agricultural products, 26 January 2005, SR 0.632.401.23, OJ L 023.

500 FDFA Bilateral Agreements Switzerland-EU, p. 6.

501 FDFA Bilateral Agreements Switzerland-EU, p. 7.

the withdrawal of one of the agreements, the other agreements – with the exception of the Research Agreement[502] – would automatically become inoperative.[503] In addition, the finalisation of these agreements established the principle of equivalence between legislation in cases where the literal adoption of the Acquis Communitaire was not a viable option.[504]

8.2.2.1 Bilateral I

These seven bilateral sectorial agreements entered into force on 1 June 2002.[505] They governed Swiss access to the EU internal market on the

502 Agreement on Scientific and Technological Cooperation between the European Communities and the European Atomic Energy Community of the one part, and the Swiss Confederation of the other part, 25 June 2007, SR 0.420.513.1 [Research Agreement]. This agreement has no longer been linked to the other six since its renewal.

503 FDFA Bilateral Agreements Switzerland-EU, p. 7.

504 There are exceptions to this rule: the Agreement between the European Communities and the Swiss Confederation on Air Transport, 20 April 2002, OJ L 114, p. 73–90 [Civil Aviation Agreement]; the Agreement between the European Union, the European Communities and the Swiss Confederation on the Swiss Confederation's Association with the Implementation, Application and Development of the Schengen Acquis (Schengen), 27 February 2008, OJ L 53; and the Agreement between the European Communities and the Swiss Confederation concerning the criteria and mechanisms for establishing the State responsible for examining a request for asylum lodged in a Member State or in Switzerland (Dublin), 27 February 2008, OJ L 53, p. 6–17.

505 See *generally*: THOMAS COTTIER/NICOLAS DIEBOLD/ISABEL KÖLLIKER/RACHEL LIECHTI-MCKEE/MATTHIAS OESCH/TETYANA PAYOSOVA/DANIEL WÜGER, Die Rechtsbeziehungen der Schweiz und der Europäischen Union, Stämpfli Verlag 2014, p. 30 *et seq* [COTTIER *et al.*]; ASTRID EPINEY, How Does European Union Law Influence Swiss Law and Policies? in: STEPHANE NAHRATH/FREDERIC VARONE, Rediscovering Public Law and Public Administration in Comparative Policy Analysis: A Tribute to Peter Knoepfel, Haupt Verlag 2009, pp. 179–196, p. 184 *et seq.*; THOMAS COTTIER/RACHEL LIECHTI-MCKEE (eds), Die Schweiz und Europa: Wirtschaftliche Integration und institutionelle Abstinez, vdf Verlag 2010.

free movement of people,[506] public procurement markets,[507] research,[508] civil aviation,[509] overland transport,[510] technical barriers to trade[511] and agriculture.[512]

8.2.2.1.1 Agriculture

This agreement is particularly important for the food sector because it aims at reducing tariff and non-tariff barriers to trade for specific product segments. Import quotas and tariff reductions apply to the cheese sector, fruit and vegetables, horticulture, meat and wine specialties.[513]

Non-tariff barriers are reduced by means of the mutual recognition of the equivalence of regulations, such as wine and spirits, organic agriculture, pest control and crop protection, fodder and seeds.[514] Since

506 Agreement between the European Communities and its Member States of the one part, and of the Swiss Confederation of the other, on the Free Movement of Persons 21 June 1999, SR 0.142.112.681. See *generally:* ASTRID EPINEY/BEATE METZ/ROBERT MOSTERS (eds), Das Personenfreizügigkeitsabkommen Schweiz-EU, Schulthess 2011; SEBASTIAN BENESCH, Das Freizügigkeitsabkommen zwischen der Schweiz und der Europäischen Gemeinschaft, Mohr Siebeck 2007; WALTER KÄLIN, 'Das bilaterale Abkommen der Schweiz mit der EG über die Freizügigkeit von Personen' (2002) Zeitschrift für Ausländerrecht und Ausländerpolitik, pp. 123–127.

507 Agreement between the European Communities and the Swiss Confederation on Certain Aspects of Government Procurement, 21 June 1999, SR 0.172.052.68.

508 Research Agreement.

509 Civil Aviation Agreement.

510 Agreement between the European Communities and the Swiss Confederation on the Carriage of Goods and Passengers by Rail and Road, 21 June 1999, SR 0.740.72.

511 Agreement between the European Communities and the Swiss Confederation on Mutual Recognition in relation to Conformity Assessment, 30 April 2002, OJ L 114.

512 Agreement between the European Communities and the Swiss Confederation on Trade in Agricultural Products, 21 June 1999, SR 0.916.026.81 [Agreement on Agriculture].

513 ROLAND NORER, Europäisierung des schweizerischen Agrarrechts: zwischen bilateralen Abkommen und autonomen Nachvollzug, in: MARTINA CARONI/SEBASTIAN HESELHAUS/KLAUS MATHIS/ROLAND NORER, Auf der Schölle und in lichten Höhen: Festschrift für Paul Richli zum 65. Geburtstag, Dike Verlag 2011, pp. 569–590.

514 ZÄCH, p. 13; FDFA Bilateral Agreements Switzerland – EU, p. 7.

2009, veterinary controls at borders were eliminated due to the recognition of the equivalence of hygiene regulations for all foodstuffs of animal origin.

8.2.2.1.2 Technical Barriers to Trade

This so-called 'Mutual Recognition Agreement' establishes the mutual recognition of conformity tests for most industrial products. It aims at eliminating the need for double conformity tests and thus provides for the legal basis to EU market access by means of the equivalence of legislation. In other words, manufacturers that carry out a conformity test in accordance with Swiss law automatically receive the required EU label to directly export and place their products on the EU market.[515]

8.2.2.2 Bilateral II

These series of agreements deal with cooperation in areas such as security, asylum, environment and culture. Relevant for the food sector is the Agreement on Processed Agricultural Products,[516] which facilitates exports for the food industry and constitutes a market liberalisation measure in the sense of the Bilateral I.

8.2.2.2.1 Processed Agricultural Products

This agreement revises Protocol II of the 1972 FTA, which regulates trade in processed agricultural products such as chocolate, cheese, pasta and pastries.

Unlike industrially produced goods, agricultural products – such as milk powder, meat products, cheese and flour – do not fall within the scope of the application of the agreements. Thus, processed goods made from agricultural commodities remained subject to two legal regimes if they constituted industrial products (subject to free trade) or were prepared with agricultural raw materials (subject to protective measures).

515 ZÄCH, p. 12; FDFA Bilateral Agreements Switzerland – EU, p. 7.

516 Agreement between the EC and the Swiss Confederation amending the Agreement between the European Economic Community and the Swiss Confederation of 22 July 1972 as regards the provisions applicable to processed agricultural products, 26 January 2005, OJ L 023.

To solve this dichotomy, Protocol II introduced a price compensation mechanism that took into account the price differences for agricultural raw materials between Switzerland and the world market. In accordance with this price difference, custom duties on imports and subsidies for exports were levied on the industrial component of these products.

The new agreement seeks to further facilitate access to the European market in as far as it simplifies the price compensation mechanism by introducing a net price compensation mechanism, which references the differences in prices between Switzerland and the corresponding EU prices. As a result of this adjustment, the EU abolished custom duties on all Swiss-processed agricultural products covered by the agreement and forwent subsidies on all products exported to Switzerland.

8.3 Swiss Food Law and the Unilateral Introduction of the Mutual Recognition Principle

Given that both parties are responsible for the implementation of the agreements, Switzerland has been adapting its legislation almost constantly to main equivalence with the EU.

Trade in foodstuffs is an area that serves well to analyse the legal framework for relations between Switzerland and the EU. In an attempt to improve the competitiveness of the Swiss market and reduce prices for consumers,[517] Switzerland unilaterally introduced the principle of mutual recognition through the revision of the Federal Act on Technical

517 COTTIER *et al.*, p. 146 *et seq*; DAVID HERREN, Das Cassis de Dijon-Prinzip im schweizerischen Recht: Gemeinsamkeiten und Divergenzen zum EU-Recht, in: THOMAS COTTIER, Die Europakompatibilität des schweizerischen Wirtschaftsrechts: Konvergenz und Divergenz, Helbing Lichtenhahn Verlag 2012, pp. 59–82; RETO HEIZMANN, Die Sonderregeln für Lebensmittel im THG: zur Legitimität der Differenzierung zwischen Lebensmitteln und anderen Produkte insbesondere unter wettbewerbsrechtlichen Gesichtspunkten, in: LEANDER LOACKER/CORINNE ZELLWEGER-GUTKNECHT (eds), Differenzierung als Legitimationsfrage, Dike Verlag 2012, pp. 331–358.

Barriers to Trade (THG)[518] and through the subsequent enactment of a detailed decree implementing it (VIPaV).[519]

It is worth emphasising that the modality of the principle of mutual recognition introduced in Switzerland applies unilaterally and to both harmonised and non-harmonised areas of food law. As a result of this, an approximation of Swiss vertical non-harmonised legislation to that of the EU appears pivotal in order to maintain the free flow of trade in foodstuffs, evidenced by the current revision at the ordinance level.

8.3.1 The Umbrella Provision in Article 16a) THG

According to the revised Article 16 THG, products may be placed on the Swiss market in two cases. They must comply with technical requirements set out in European legislation or in the legislation of a Member State.[520] Also, the product in question must be placed on a market regulated by those fulfilled technical requirements.[521] The main challenge that this provision poses is how to avoid in a worst-case scenario a decline in food quality standards due to allegedly less stringent rules at the production and manufacture stages outside Switzerland.

A well-known judgement of the ECJ, *Pistre*[522] illustrates the fears Swiss producers in particular may have in accepting the unilateral introduction of the mutual recognition principle through the modified THG. Although no judicial precedent for Switzerland, this case may serve as legal inspiration when assessing the effectiveness of the new rule. In this case, a French producer of 'mountain ham' was prosecuted for failure

518 Swiss Federal Act on Technical Barriers to Trade, *ger.* Bundesgesetz vom 6. Oktober 1995 über die technischen Handelshemmnissen, SR 946.51 [THG].

519 Swiss Federal Decree on the placement on the market of products manufactured according to foreign technical standards and their control in in the market, *ger.* Veordnung über das Inverkehrbringen von nach ausländischen technischen Vorschriften hergestellten Produkten und über deren Überwachung auf dem Markt (VIPaV), 19 May 2010, SR 946.513.8.

520 Art. 16a)1.a) THG.

521 Art. 16a)1.b) THG.

522 Christian Poucet v. Assurances Générales de France and Caisse Mutuelle Régionale du Languedoc-Roussillon [1997] Case C-321/94, Judgment of 7 May 1997, ECR I 2343 [Pistre].

to comply with national rules on ham quality. Yet these same rules were not being implemented for imported mountain ham because the administrative authorities realised that it would not comply with EU law.[523] The Court argued that the French food quality rules in question offered a marketing advantage to domestic products, given that the requirements were so strictly defined that only French producers could comply with them.[524]

Likewise, the European Court of Justice decided in the German Quality Products Case[525] that the right to affix a mark onto German goods (if certain requirements were complied with) amounted to a discriminatory marketing scheme. This was due to the impossibility of foreign products to opt for this quality mark.[526]

Were the ECJ case law binding for Switzerland, the question of the extent to which national laws should regulate quality in food would already be solved. So long as domestic quality schemes provide for a *de iure* or *de facto* marketing advantage for national products, they are not compatible with EU law. As a result, Switzerland would have to opt for a different method than mandatory or voluntary standards to guarantee high quality food products in order to avoid the risk of being challenged before the ECJ.

8.3.2 The Non-Discrimination Clause in Article 16b) THG

This provision aims at avoiding reverse discrimination of Swiss producers by allowing them to choose between compliance with Swiss technical requirement and those of an EU Member State, as long as they produce for the domestic market.[527] This modification undoubtedly poses difficult questions concerning legal enforcement. Swiss official control

523 Pistre, para. 46.

524 Pistre, para. 45. See *also*: CHALMERS *et al.*, pp. 755–756.

525 Commission of the European Communities v. Federal Republic of Germany [2002] Case C-325/00, Judgment of 5 November 2002, ECR I-9977 [German Quality Products Case].

526 CHALMERS *et al.*, p. 758.

527 Art. 16b) THG states: 'Manufacturers in Switzerland that only produce for the domestic market, may place on the market their products manufactured according to Art. 16.a) 1.a' [unofficial translation].

authorities will not only need to be acquainted with national technical standards, but also with all the EU Member States' technical standards that a Swiss producer may decide to produce upon. The burden of proof seems to rest with the public authorities.[528]

8.3.3 The Exception for Foodstuffs in Article 16c) THG

Imported or domestic foodstuffs that do not comply with Swiss technical standards need first of all authorisation from the Federal Office of Public Health in order to be placed on the Swiss market.[529] This is so even if it can be shown that one or more of the EU Member States' technical requirements have been complied with. In fact, compliance with one of EU Member States' technical standards is a prerequisite for the granting of an authorisation. Once the producer has shown that the product at issue complies with a certain set of EU rules and that it has been placed on the EU internal market before, the authorities will proceed to authorise its import into Switzerland. This positive list requirement does not seem to exceed the margin of appreciation that national authorities retain in matters subject to non-harmonised areas of EU Law.

8.4 Conclusion

While the unilateral introduction of the mutual recognition principle has improved the legal framework of trade relations, the revised THG poses various practical challenges for domestic rules still in force.

This chapter has illustrated one concrete example of regulatory equivalence by examining the Swiss adoption of the European principle of mutual recognition for trade in food. In doing so, section II described the applicable legal framework to trade in foodstuffs between Switzerland

528 It is being currently discussed at the federal level (files with the author) with no unanimous view. The confusion among official control representatives is apparent.

529 Art. 16c) THG.

and the EU. It first examined the 1972 FTA to later focus on the food relevant aspects of the Bilateral Agreements. Section III analysed the current applicable legal framework to trade in food between Switzerland and the EU, pointing out the benefits and challenges of a unilateral adoption of European equivalence. Bearing in mind that the EU does not recognise as equivalent a particular Swiss food legislation and given the judicial precedents set by the ECJ, a formula that guarantees the free movement of goods and the assurance of high Swiss food quality standards remains to be found.

Conclusion: Implications of Food Safety and Quality Standards in International Trade Law

New governance mechanisms have rapidly evolved to ensure that global food demands are met. The result is an increasingly complex network of food safety and quality standards influencing international trade law that are at times difficult to navigate. In addition, the rise of informal rules complementing treaty law in international trade can hardly be overseen, particularly when it comes to the proliferation of international food standards.[530]

This research aimed at mapping the legal aspects of the current global architecture for food governance. In doing so, it conceptualized global food governance following a grounded theory approach, whereby the validity of descriptions was constantly updated through comparative methods of document analysis. It followed that global food governance could be identified as a regulatory framework involving non-binding standards and rules, public-private cooperation and self-regulation through guidelines and recommendations, that is ever changing and thus, continues to trigger new forms of governance – through harmonization, cooperation and equivalence methods. Based on these results, it presented a comprehensive legal framework of food safety and quality standards that responds to the underlying research question about the legal implications of food safety and quality standards for international trade law. Six main legal findings conclude with work, and are identified as follows.

530 PAUWELYN, Rule-Based Trade 2.0, pp. 5,14.

1. Legal Finding Nr. 1: Food quality regulation based on international standards is *prima facie* compliant with the TBT Agreement

Domestic regulation based on recognized international standards will benefit from a rebuttable presumption of compliance with the TBT Agreement, shifting the burden of proof to the Claimant.

The question of whether market access constitutes the ultimate goal of regulation by implementing the theory of competitive advantage was tested against the backdrop posed by the relevant economic theories of international trade, followed by an examination of the impact of market failures, particularly information asymmetry, in the creation of trade rules. After the establishment of the WTO and with a shift towards deep integration trade rules aiming at harmonisation, the importance of the current multilateral trading system in solving disputes arising out of divergent standards is apparent. As such, an understanding of the most relevant legal principles of WTO law is necessary in order to establised their implications for food standardisation. National Treatment, MFN Treatment, the concept of like products and general exceptions constitute the foundations of all WTO instruments, and are all enshrined in the WTO Agreements, including the TBT Agreement, the SPS Agreement and the TRIPS Agreement.[531]

Although voluntary in nature, food standards are vested of a legally binding character by reference to the presumption of compliance implicit in the WTO Agreements. It is however the jurisprudence based on the TBT Agreement that best captured the legal concept of international standard to assess the conformity of domestic food measures with WTO members' international law obligations. The benchmark offered by Article 2.4 proves useful to test the legality of prima facie protectionist technical regulations.

Based on four leading cases, the WTO Appellate Body first developed a two-tier test that conceptualises 'relevant international standards'. Significantly, the conformity test in Article 2.4 of the TBT Agreement is far from precise. However, the interpretative path developed by the WTO

531 See *supra*, Chapter 1.

Appellate Body offers increased certainty as to the extents to which the relevant stakeholders and governments may rely on voluntary food standards to comply with international legal obligations.[532]

2. Legal Finding Nr. 2: Food standards designed by international standard-setting bodies as established in Legal Finding 1 acquired a *de facto* mandatory effect post-WTO establishment

As a result of legal finding Nr. 1, the role played by international standard-setting bodies in the creation of new forms of food governance (rules, standards, guidelines and recommendations) dramatically increased. The CAC and the ISO, as the two most relevant standard-setting bodies for international trade in food, were examined and compared. Particularly important are the legal mechanisms governing the development and adoption of standards, as well as their rules of procedure. The importance given to membership openness in international standard-setting bodies, as defined by the Appellate Body in US Tuna II (Mexico), highlighted the need to assess membership mechanisms. While this aspect is undisputed in so far as the CAC is concerned, until recently the legal status of ISO membership was uncertain. The situation changed after an amendment of its Statutes was adopted in 2012, whereby individuals and companies are no longer eligible for ISO membership. Although the relevant international standards are devised by global experts, it is only after their implementation at the domestic level that they become effective. As an illustrative example, the legal mechanisms and judicial relevance of the Food Code Commission in Germany were analysed to give a context to the challenges posed by consensus-driven standard-setting bodies.

While the importance of international (food) standards appears undisputed to date, the legal architecture to which they are subject is not yet clear. The quality of foodstuffs is likely to qualify as a product characteristic and thus, the rules governing technical requirements in international

532 See *supra*, Chapter 2.

trade also apply. The TBT Agreement provides a legal definition of technical regulation that has been assessed in the light of established WTO Case Law. As such, it is here argued that the elevated status attributed to the ISO has the potential to extend the scope of application of the TBT Agreement to virtually all actors involved in an international (food) trade transaction.[533]

3. Legal Finding Nr. 3: Private voluntary food safety standards fall within the scope of application of the SPS Agreement only in cases where they are adopted by international standard-setting bodies as established in Legal Finding 2

It is undisputed that differing food safety standards arising from divergent regulatory approaches may impose important non-tariff barriers to trade in foodstuffs. The legal implications of food safety standards are thus far-reaching. Since the inception of the WTO, the SPS Agreement has been providing an effective legal framework to assess the legality of domestic food safety rules. Its most relevant principles, such as the obligation to base SPS measures on science, the precautionary principle and equivalence, were identified and examined. The widely disputed use of private food safety standards provided the basis for a case study on the applicability of the SPS Agreement to non-governmental actors in food trade. It addressed the possible legal status of such private SPS measures and the endeavors undertaken by Members within the SPS Committee. Although five actions were agreed years ago, Members continue to struggle with the adoption of the first one. It remains to be seen whether the deadlock will be broken any time soon.[534]

533 See *supra*, Chapter 3.

534 See *supra*, Chapter 6.

4. Legal Finding Nr. 4: Food quality labelling standards trigger the protection of the TRIPS Agreement to increase consumer information

Likewise, consumer and market demands have long played an essential role in triggering the proliferation of food standards because their purpose is to indicate that foodstuffs are of a certain origin, material, and quality. Labelling has proved the most efficient tool to guarantee food quality and thus, it may easily become a *de facto* obstacle to market access. The conflict between trademark rights and consumer protection has its origins in incepted dynamics well preceding the establishment of the WTO.[535]

Trademarks are tools to guarantee food quality. The TRIPS Agreement provides a comprehensive legal framework against which the conformity of food labelling standards may be assessed for WTO compliance. In doing so, this work identified what constituted a trademark, analysing the peculiarities of its characteristics and functions under Article 15.1 of the TRIPS Agreement. The analysis then focused on the rights conferred to trademark owners, their attributed presumption of absoluteness, as well as the protection afforded against confusion under Article 16.1 of the TRIPS Agreement. The exceptions to these conferred trademark rights were scrutinised in the light of Article 17 and its interpretative jurisprudence, whereby a three-tier compliance test was developed by the WTO Appellate Body. Lastly, an analysis of the special trademark requirements under Article 20 of the TRIPS Agreement concluded that the threshold established therein is considerably lower than that provided in the limited exceptions clause of Article 17.[536]

535 See *supra*, Chapter 4.
536 See *supra*, Chapter 5.

5. Legal Finding Nr. 5: Food standards subject to non-harmonised areas of EU law are more likely to display trade-distorting effects

The need for mandatory quality standards is essential in order to determine whether a product can be lawfully placed on a particular (European) market. After the entering into force of Reg. (EC) Nr. 764/2008, and in the light of ECJ Case Law, however, the costs of maintaining and enforcing national quality standards in non-harmonised areas of Food Law have increased. Conversely, technical rules on the composition of foodstuffs are subject to deeper legal scrutiny each time the competent authority of a Member State renders an administrative decision regarding a product lawfully marketed in another Member State.

The European regulatory framework for foodstuffs provided an example of standard coordination. EU principles underlying the free movement of goods were the object of study, where the different regulatory approaches applied in recent decades were identified and analysed. An analysis of leading ECJ Case Law. laid the foundation for the creation of one of the pillars of EU Internal Market Law: the principle of mutual recognition.

The development of the mutual recognition principle has undoubtedly promoted free movement of goods, while at the same time gradually dismantling trade barriers between Member States. This deduction has been made throughout this thesis while examining the European regulatory system applicable to trade. It concluded that the mutual recognition principle is the most efficient available means of ensuring the free movement of foodstuffs subject to non-harmonised rules within the EU.[537]

537 See *supra*, Chapter 7.

6. Legal Finding Nr. 6: The equivalence of food standards between the EU and Switzerland as established in Legal Finding 5 poses practical challenges that render its effective enforcement non-viable

As the legal principles laid out in the analysed WTO instruments influence regional legislation, so does regional legislation influence domestic orders. The final chapter addressed the implications of European Food Law in Swiss legislation governing the trade in foodstuffs. In doing this, it illustrated regulatory equivalence of food standards by examining the Swiss adoption of the European principle of mutual recognition for trade in food.

While the unilateral introduction of the mutual recognition principle has improved the legal framework of trade relations, the revised THG poses various practical challenges for domestic rules still in force. Bearing in mind that the EU does not recognise as equivalent a particular Swiss food legislation and given the judicial precedents set by the ECJ, a formula that guarantees the free movement of goods and the assurance of high Swiss food quality standards remains to be found.[538]

In the course of the legal analysis carried out in the thesis at hand, the hypothesis that food quality and safety implications new forms of global governance – such as rules, standards, guidelines and recommendations – have acquired a prominent place in the legal architecture of rules governing trade in food, and have thus triggered the creation of new forms of governance designed to meet the demands of food producers and global food markets, has been proved based on three regulatory approaches: harmonisation (WTO), cooperation (EU) and mutual recognition or equivalence (Switzerland). While focusing on the existing jurisprudence dealing with food measures, this works concludes that the normative nature of food standards does not constitute a determining factor in assessing the applicability of the relevant international trade instruments. In spite of this, the trade-distorting effects displayed by

538 See *supra*, Chapter 8.

divergent domestic measures on food safety and quality can only be reduced through effective regulatory strategies that aim at harmonizing trade rules while maintaining state regulatory autonomy. There is a balance to be struck in the application of all relevant international trade agreements to safeguard legitimate aims and guarantee market liberalization. The new emerging forms of global food governance, albeit very different in nature and extent, provide additional tools to enhance the effectiveness of domestic food legal frameworks , which in turn are less likely to cause a detrimental effect on compliance with international trade obligations. Although consumer protection and health preservation remain valid objectives to be pursued, the facilitation of food trade through a coherent set of international rules appears essential, rather than detrimental, to the global economy.

Bibliography

ABBOTT, FREDERICK, 'WTO Dispute Settlement and the Agreement on Trade-Related Aspects of Intellectual Property Rights' in: PETERSMANN, ERNST-ULRICH (ed), International Trade Law and the GATT/WTO Dispute Settlement System, Kluwer Law International 1997, pp. 413–437.

ACKERLOF, GEORGE, 'The Market for "Lemons": Quality Uncertainties and the Market Mechanism' (1970) 84 Quarterly Journal of Economics, pp. 488–500.

ALEMANNO, ALBERTO, 'Food Safety and the Single European Market' in: VOGEL, DAVID/ANSELL, CHRISTOPH, What's the Beef? The Contested Governance of European Food Safety, MIT Press 2006, pp. 237–258.

ALEMANNO, ALBERTO, Trade in Food: Regulatory and Judicial Approaches in the EC and the WTO, Cameron May 2007.

ALIKHAN, SHAHID/MASHELKAR, RAGHUNATH, Intellectual Property and Competitive Strategies in the 21st Century, 2nd ed., Kluwer Law International 2009.

ANDERMAN, STEVEN, The Interface between Intellectual Property Rights and Competition Law, Cambridge University Press 2007.

APPLETON, ARTHUR, 'Conformity Assessment Procedures' in: EPPS, TRACEY/TREBILCOCK, MICHAEL (eds), Research Handbook on the WTO and Technical Barriers to Trade, Edward Elgar 2013, pp. 81–119.

BARNARD CATHERINE, The Substantive Law of the EU, 4th ed., Oxford University Press 2013.

BARRETT, MARGRETH, 'Reconciling Fair Use and Trademark Use' (2010) 28 (1) Cardozo Arts & Entertainment, pp. 1–64.

BAUMGARTNER, TOBIAS, 'Allgemeiner Regelungsrahmen im EU-Lebensmittelrecht' in: WEBER ROLF/KLEMM URS/BAUMGARTNER TOBIAS/GROLIMUND NINA/TRÜTEN DIRK, Lebensmittelrecht EU-Schweiz, 2nd ed., Schulthess 2012, pp. 53–76.

BAUMGARTNER, TOBIAS/UEBE, WESSELINA, 'European Union' in: KIRCHSTEIGER-MEIER EVELYN/BAUMGARTNER TOBIAS (eds), Global Food Legislation: An Overview, Wiley Publishing 2014, pp. 111–142.

BEAS RODRIGUEZ JR, EDSON, The General Exceptions Clauses of the TRIPS Agreement: Promoting Sustainable Development, Cambridge University Press 2012.

BELSON, JEFFREY, Certification Marks, Sweet & Maxwell 2002.

BENESCH, SEBASTIAN, Das Freizügigkeitsabkommen zwischen der Schweiz und der Europäischen Gemeinschaft, Mohr Siebeck 2007.

BERNARD NICHOLAS, 'On the Art of Not Mixing One's Drinks: Dassonville and Cassis de Dijon Revisited' in: MADURO MIGUEL/AZOULAI LOIC (eds), The Past and Future of EU Law, Hart Publishing 2001, pp. 456–464.

BOAS, MORTEN, 'Governance as Multilateral Bank Policy: The Cases of the African Development Bank and the Asian Development Bank' (1998) 10 (2) European Journal of Development Research, pp. 117–134.

BREUSS, FRITZ/COTTIER, THOMAS/MÜLLER-GRAFF, PETER-CHRISTIAN (eds), Die Schweiz im Europäischen Integrationsprozess, Helbing Liechtehahn Verlag 2008.

BUSCH, LAWRENCE, 'The Moral Economic of Grades and Standards' (2000) 16 Journal of Rural Studies, pp. 273–283.

CERNY, PHILIPP, 'Globalization and the Changing Logic of Collective Action' (1995) 49 (4) International Organizations, pp. 595–621.

CHALMERS, DAVID, 'Private Power and Public Authority in European Union Law' (2005–6) 8 Cambridge Yearbook of European Legal Studies, pp. 59–94.

CHALMERS, DAMIAN/DAVIES, GARETH/MONTI, GIORGIO, European Union Law: Cases and Materials, 2nd ed., Cambridge University Press 2010.

CHARNOVITZ, STEVE, International Standards and the WTO, The George Washington University Law School Public Law and Legal Theory Working Paper Nr. 133, May 2002.

CHEW, DONALD, Studies in International Corporate Finance and Governance Systems – A Comparison of the US, Japan and Europe, Oxford University Press 1997.

CODEX ALIMENTARIUS COMMISSION (CAC), This is Codex Alimentarius, 1995.

CODEX ALIMENTARIUS COMMISSION (CAC), Understanding The Codex Alimentarius, 3rd ed., WHO/FAO, Rome 2006.

COHEN, AMICHAI, 'Bureaucratic Internationalization: Domestic Governmental Agencies and the Legitimization of International Law' (2005) 30 Georgetown Journal of International Law, pp. 1079–1144.

COHEN JEHORAM, TOBIAS/VAN NISPEN, CONSTANT/HUYDECOPER, TONY, European Trademark Law: Community Trademark Law and Harmonized National Trademark Law, Wolters Kluwer 2010.

COLBERT, JEAN-BAPTISTE, Memorandum on Trade, 1664, reprinted by KRAUS, NENDELN (Lichtenstein), 1979.

COMMISSION ON GLOBAL GOVERNANCE, Our Global Neighborhood, Oxford University Press 1995.

CORREA, CARLOS, Trade Related Aspects of Intellectual Property Rights: A Commentary on the TRIPS Agreement, Oxford University Press 2007.

COTTIER, THOMAS, 'Risk Management Experience in WTO Dispute Settlement' in: ROBERTSON, DAVID/KELLOW, AYNSLEY (eds), Globalization and the Environment: Risk Assessment in the WTO, Edward Elgar 2011, pp. 41–66.

COTTIER, THOMAS/MEITINGER, INGO, The TRIPS Agreement without a Competition Agreement?, Fondazione Eni Enrico Mettei, Trade and Competition in the WTO and Beyond, Venice 1998.

COTTIER, THOMAS/OESCH, MATTHIAS, International Trade Regulation: Law and Policy in the WTO, the European Union and Switzerland: Cases, Materials and Comments, Stämpfli 2005.

COTTIER, THOMAS/DIEBOLD, NICOLAS/KÖLLIKER, ISABEL/LIECHTI-MCKEE, RACHEL/OESCH, MATTHIAS/PAYOSOVA, TETYANA/WÜGER, DANIEL, Die Rechtsbeziehungen der Schweiz und der Europäischen Union, Stämpfli Verlag 2014.

COTTIER, THOMAS/LIECHTI-MCKEE, RACHEL (ed), Die Schweiz und Europa: Wirtschaftliche Integration und institutionelle Abstinez, vdf Verlag 2010.

COURVILLE, SASHA/PARKER, CHRISTINE/WATCHIRS, HELEN, 'Introduction: Auditing in Regulatory Perspective' (2003) 25 (3) Law & Policy, pp. 179–184.

CRAIG, PAUL/DE BÚRCA, GRAINNE, EU Law – Text, Cases and Materials, 5th ed., Oxford University Press, 2011.

CUNNINGHAM, WILLIAM, The Growth of English Industry and Commerce during the Early and Middle Ages, Cambridge, At the University Press 1882.

DAVIES, GARETH, 'Is Mutual Recognition an Alternative to Harmonisation: Lessons on Trade and Tolerance of Diversity from the EU' in: ORTINO, FEDERICO/BARTELS, LORAND (eds), Regional Trade Agreements and the WTO, Oxford University Press 2006, pp. 265–280.

DE BURCA, GRAINNE/KEOHANE, ROBERT/SABEL, CHARLES, New Modes of Pluralist Global Governance, New York University, School of Law, Public Law and Legal Theory Research Paper Working Series, Working Paper Nr. 13–08, March 2013.

DESAI, MEGHNAD/REDFERN, PAUL (eds), Global Governance: Ethics and Economics of the World Order, Printer 1995.

DIEHL PAUL (ed), The Politics of Global Governance: International Organizations in an Independent World, Lynne Rienner 1997.

DINWOODIE, GRAEME/DREYFUSS, ROCHELLE, A Neofederalist Vision of TRIPS: The Resilience of the International Intellectual Property Regime, Oxford University Press 2012.

DREXL, JOSEF, Research Handbook on Intellectual Property and Competition Law, Edward Elgar Publishing 2010.

EGAN, MICHELLE, Constructing a European Market: Standards, Regulation and Governance, Oxford University Press 2001.

EPINEY, ASTRID, 'How Does European Union Law Influence Swiss Law and Policies?' in: NAHRATH, STEPHANE/VARONE, FREDERIC, Rediscovering Public Law and Public Administration in Comparative Policy Analysis: A Tribute to Peter Knoepfel, Haupt Verlag 2009, pp. 179–195.

EPINEY, ASTRID/METZ, BEATE/MOSTERS, ROBERT, Das Personenfreizügigkeitsabkommen Schweiz-EU, Schulthess 2011.

EPPS, TRACEY, International Trade and Health Protection: A Critical Assessment of the WTO's SPS Agreement, Edward Elgar 2008.

EPPS, TRACEY/TREBILCOCK, MICHAEL, Research Handbook of the WTO and Technical Barriers to Trade, Edward Elgar Publishing 2013.

EVERSON, MICHELL/VOS, ELLEN, 'The Scientification of Politics and the Politisation of Science' in: EVERSON MICHELL/VOS ELLEN (eds), Uncertain Risks Regulated, Routledge-Cavendish 2009, pp. 1–18.

FALK, RICHARD, On Humane Governance, Penn State Press 1995.

FEZER, KARL-HEINZ, Markenrecht, 4th, ed. C.H. Beck 2009.

FLETCHER, IAN, Free Trade Doesn't Work: What Should Replace It and Why, US Business and Industry Council 2011.

FOLTEA, MARINA, International Organizations in WTO Dispute Settlement: How Much Sensitivity?, Cambridge University Press 2012.

FUCHS, DORIS/KALFAGIANNI, AGNI/HAVINGA, TETTY, 'Actors in Private Food Governance: The Legitimacy of Retail Standards and Multistakeholders Initiatives with Civil Society Participation' (2011) 28 (3) Agricultural Human Values, pp. 353–367.

FULPONI, LINDA, Private Standards Schemes and Developing Countries Access to Global Value Chains: Challenges and Opportunities Emerging from Four Case Studies, OECD, August 2007.

FULPONI, LINDA, 'Private Voluntary Standards in the Food System: The Perspective of Major Food Retailers in OECD Countries' (2006) 31 Food Policy, pp. 1–13.

GARCIA, GENARO/CARRUTH, REBA, 'Multilateral Governance of Food Safety in Global Food Industries and Food Systems: The Role of FAO, WHO and Codex Alimentarius in Regulatory Harmonization' in: CARRUTH REBA (ed), Global Governance of Food and Agriculture Industries: Transatlantic Regulatory Harmonization and Multilateral Policy Cooperation for Food Safety, Edward Elgar 2006, pp. 392–430.

GAVA, ROY/VARONE, FREDERIC, 'So Close, Yet so Far? The EU's Footprint in Swiss Legislative Legislation' in: BROUARD, SYLVAIN/COSTA, OLIVIER/KÖNIG, THOMAS (eds), The Europeanization of Domestic Legislation: The Empirical Implications of the Delors' Myth in Nine Countries, Springer 2012, pp. 197–221.

GERLACH, CHRISTIAN, 'Illusions of Global Governance: Transnational Agribusiness inside the UN System' in: NÜTZENADEL, ALEXANDER/TRENTMANN, FRANK, Food and Globalization: Consumption, Markets and Politics in the Modern World, Berg Publishers 2008, pp. 193–211.

GERVAIS, DANIEL, The TRIPS Agreement – Drafting History and Analysis, 3rd ed., Sweet & Maxwell 2008.

GHIDINI, GUSTAVO, Intellectual Property and Competition Law: The Innovation Nexus, Edward Elgar Publishing 2006.

GIUSTI, ANNA/BIGNETTI, ENRICO/CANELLA, CARLO, 'Exploring New Frontiers in Total Food Quality Definition and Assessment: from Chemical to Neurochemical Properties' (2008) 1 (2) Food and Bioprocess Technology, pp. 130–142.

GORMLEY, LAURENCE, 'Cassis de Dijon and the Communication from the Commission' (1981) 6 European Law Review, pp. 454–459.

GREY PAUL, 'Food Law and the Internal Market: Taking Stock' (1990) 15 (2) Food Policy, pp. 111–121.

GROVES, PETER (ed), Sourcebook on Intellectual Property Law, Cavendish Publishing 1997.

GRUSZCZYNSKI, LUCASZ, Regulating Health and Environmental Risks under WTO Law: A Critical Analysis of the SPS Agreement, Oxford University Press 2010.

HAGENMEYER, MORITZ, 'Modern Food Safety Requirements – According to EC Regulation 178/2002' (2002) 4 Zeitschrift für das gesamte Lebensmittelrecht, pp. 443–459.

HATANAKA, MAKI, 'Assessing Rule-Based Governance Mechanisms in an Era of Scientism' (2011) 25 (3) Journal of Rural Sciences, pp. 141–159.

HAVINGA, TETTY, 'Private Regulation of Food Safety by Supermarkets' (2006) 28 (4) Law and Policy 28, pp. 515–533.

HEIZMANN, RETO, 'Die Sonderregeln für Lebensmittel im THG: zur Legitimität der Differenzierung zwischen Lebensmitteln und anderen Produkte insbesondere unter wettbewerbsrechtlichen Gesichtspunkten' in: LOACKER, LEANDER/ZELLWEGER-GUTKNECHT, CORINNE (eds), Differenzierung als Legitimationsfrage, Dike Verlag 2012, pp. 331–358.

HELD, DAVID, Global Transformation, Stanford University Press 1999.

HELFER, LAURENCE, 'Regime Shifting: The TRIPS Agreement and New Dynamics of International Intellectual Property Lawmaking' (2004) 29 (1) Yale Journal of International Law, pp. 1–83.

HENSON, SPENCER/REARDON, THOMAS, 'Private Agri-Food Standards: Implications for Food Policy and the Agri-Food System' (2005) 30 Food Policy, pp. 241–253.

HERDEGEN, MATTHIAS, 'Biotechnology and Regulatory Risk Assessment' in: BERMANN, GEORGE/HERDEGEN, MATTHIAS/LINDSETH, PETER (eds), Transatlantic Regulatory Cooperation: Legal Problems and Political Prospects, Oxford University Press 2001, pp. 301–317.

HERREN, DAVID, 'Das Cassis de Dijon-Prinzip im schweizerischen Recht: Gemeinsamkeiten und Divergenzen zum EU-Recht' in: COTTIER, THOMAS, Die Europakompatibilität des schweizerischen Wirtschaftsrechts: Konvergenz und Divergenz, Helbing Lichtenhahn Verlag 2012, pp. 59–82.

HEWSON, MARTIN/SINCLAIR, TIMOTHY, 'The Emergence of Global Governance Theory' in: HEWSON, MARTIN/SINCLAIR, TIMOTHY (eds), Global Governance Theory, State University of New York 1999, pp. 11–30.

HILTY, RETO, 'Individual, Multiple and Collective Ownership: What Impact on Competition?' in: ROSEN, JAN (ed), Individualism and Collectiveness in Intellectual Property Law, Edward Elgar Publishing 2012, pp. 3–44.

HOBBS, JILL, 'Public and Private Standards for Food Safety and Quality: International Trade Implications' (2010) 11 (1) The Estey Centre Journal of International Law and Trade Policy, pp. 136–152.

HOLLERAN, ERIN/BREDAHL, MAURY/ZAIBET, LOKMAN, 'Private Incentives for Adopting Food Safeyt and Quality Assurance' (2004) 24 (6) Food Policy, pp. 669–683.

HORN, HENRIK/WEILER, JOSEPH, 'European Communities – Trade Description of Sardines: Textualism and its Discontent' in: HORN, HENRIK/MAVROIDIS, PETROS (eds), The WTO Case Law of 2002, Cambridge University Press 2005, pp. 248–275.

HOWSE, ROBERT, A New Device for Creating International Legal Normativity: The WTO Technical Barriers to Trade Agreement and 'International Standards', in: JOERGES, CHRISTIAN/PETERSMANN, ERNST-ULRICH (eds), Constitutionalism, Multilevel Trade Governance and Social Regulation, Hart Publishing 2006, pp. 383–395.

HOWSE, ROBERT/NICOLAIDIS, KALYPSO, 'Enhancing WTO Legitimacy: Constitutionalization or Global Subsidiarity?' (2003) 16 Governance, pp. 73–94.

HYDEN, GORAN, 'Governance and the Study of Politics' in: HYDEN, GORAN/BRATTON, MICHAEL (eds), Governance and Politics in Africa, Lynne Rienner 1992, pp. 1–26.

IRWIN, DOUGLAS, Against the Tide: An Intellectual History of Free Trade, Princeton University Press, 1996.

INTERNATIONAL STANDARDISATION ORGANISATION (ISO), Friendship Among Equals: Recollection from ISO's First Fifty Years, ISO 1997.

JAFFE, STEVE/MASAKURE, OLIVIER, 'Strategic Use of Private Standards to Enhance International Competitiveness: Vegetable Exports from Kenya and Elsewhere' (2005) 30 Food Policy, pp. 316–333.

JOERGES, CHRISTIAN, 'Integration through De-legalisation?' (2008) 33 European Law Review, pp. 291–312.

JOINT FAO/WHO FOOD STANDARDS PROGRAM, 'Assuring Food Safety and Quality: Guidelines for Strengthening National Food Control Systems' FAO Food and Nutrition Paper Nr. 76, Rome 2003.

JOINT FAO/WHO FOOD STANDARDS PROGRAM, Codex Alimentarius Commission, Procedural Manual, 19th ed., Rome 2010.

KÄLIN, WALTER, 'Das bilaterale Abkommen der Schweiz mit der EG über die Freizügigkeit von Personen' (2002) Zeitschrift für Ausländerrecht und Ausländerpolitik, pp. 123–127.

KEITH, VINCENT, 'Mad Cows and Eurocrats – Community Responses to the BSE Crisis' (2004) 10 (5) European Law Journal, pp. 499–517.

KELLERHALS, ANDREAS/BAUMGARTNER, TOBIAS, 'Das Cassis-de-Dijon-Prinzip und die Schweiz' (2006) 102 Schweizerische Juristenzeitung, pp. 321–330.

KELLERHALS, ANDREAS/BAUMGARTNER, TOBIAS, A Different Neighborhood Policy: Switzerland's Approach to European Integration, Schulthess 2014.

KOOIMAN, JAN, 'Findings, Recommendations and Speculations' in: KOOIMAN, JAN (ed), Modern Governance: New Government-Society Interactions, Sage 1993, pp. 249–262.

KRAPOHL, SEBASTIAN, 'Risk Regulation in the EU between interests and expertise – The Case of BSE' (2003) 10 Journal of European Public Policy, pp. 189–207.

KRAPOHL, SEBASTIAN, 'Thalidomide, BSE, and the Single Market: An Historical-Institutionalist Approach to Regulatory Regimes in the European Union' (2007) 46 European Journal of Political Research, pp. 25–46.

KRUGMAN, PAUL, Strategic Trade Policy and the New International Economics, MIT Press 1986.

KRUGMAN, PAUL, 'Is Free Trade Passe?' (1987) 1 (2) Journal of Economic Perspectives, pp. 131–144.

KRUGMAN, PAUL, 'The Narrow and Broad Arguments for Free Trade' (1993) 83 (2) The American Economic Review, pp. 362–266.

KUDRYAVTSEV, ARKADY, 'The TBT Agreement in Context' in: EPPS, TRACEY/TREBILCOCK, MICHAEL, Research Handbook of the WTO and Technical Barriers to Trade, Edward Elgar Publishing 2013, pp. 17–80.

LANDES, WILLIAM/POSNER, RICHARD, The Economic Structure of Intellectual Property Law, Harvard University Press 2003.

LANG, ANDREW, World Trade Law after Neoliberalism: Reimagining the Global Economic Order, Oxford University Press 2011.

LATHAM, ROBERT, 'Politics in a Floating World' in: HEWSON, MARTIN/SINCLAIR, TIMOTHY (eds), Global Governance Theory, State University of New York Press 1999.

LAWRENCE, ROBERT, 'Comment on Gary C. Hufbauer' in: SIEBERT, HORST (ed), Global Governance: An Architecture for the World Economy, Springer 2003, pp. 270–274.

LESTER, SIMON/MERCURIO, BRYAN/DAVIES, ARWEL/LEITNER, KARA, World Trade Law, Hart Publishing 2008.

LESTER, SIMON/STEMBERG, WILLIAM, 'The GATT Origins of TBT Agreement Article 2.1 and 2.2' (2014) 17 (1) Journal of International Economic Law, pp. 215–232.

LIVERMORE, MICHAEL, 'Authority and Legitimacy in Global Governance: Deliberation, Institutional Differentiation and the Codex Alimentarius' (2006) 81 New York University Law Review, pp. 766–801.

LOCONTO, ALLISON/BUSCH, LAWRENCE, 'Standards, Techno-Economic Networks, and Playing Fields: Performing the Global Market Economy' (2010) 17 Review of International Political Economy, pp. 507–36.

LOYA, THOMAS/BOLI, JOHN, 'Standardization in the World Policy: Technical Rationality over Power' in: BOLI JOHN/THOMAS GEORGE (eds), Constructing World Culture, Stanford University Press 1999, pp. 169–197.

MACRORY, PATRICK/APPLETON, ARTHUR/PLUMMER, MICHAEL (eds), The World Trade Organization: Legal, Economic and Political Analysis, Vol. I, Springer 2005.

MAIDANA-ELETTI, MARIELA, 'Market Access and Trademark Protection in the WTO Regime: The Case of Certification Marks' in: SCHLÄPFER, LEA/ZAUGG, HELENA (eds), Recht und Gesundheit, Schulthess 2013, pp. 69–86.

MAIDANA-ELETTI MARIELA, 'Trade in Foodstuffs: The Impact of EU Internal Market Rules on Swiss Food Legislation' in: MAIDANA-ELETTI, MARIELA/TOEPKE, CARLY, Recht und Gesellschaft, Schulthess 2014, pp. 141–166.

MAIDANA-ELETTI, MARIELA, 'International Food Standards and WTO Law' (2014) 19 (2) Deakin Law Review, pp. 217–241.

MAIDANA-ELETTI, MARIELA, 'Food Labelling and Trademark Law' in: RÜDIGER WOLFRUM (ed), Max Planck Encyclopedia of Public International Law, Oxford University Press 2015.

MANN, RICHARD/ROBERTS, BARRY, Smith and Roberson's Business Law, 14th ed., South-Western Cengage Learning 2009.

MATTHEE, MARIELLE, 'The Codex Alimentarius Commission and its Food Safety Measures in the Light of their New Status' in: EVERSON MICHELLE/VOS ELLEN (eds), Uncertain Risks Regulated, Routledge Cavendish 2009, pp. 323–344.

MAVROIDIS, PETROS, Trade in Goods, Oxford University Press 2007.

MCCARTHY, JAMES/PRUDHAM, SCOOT, 'Neoliberal Nature and the Nature of Neoliberalism' (2004) 35 (3) Geoforum 35, pp. 275–283.

MCCLUSKEY, JILL/WINFREE, JASON, 'Pre-Empting Public Regulation with Private Food Quality Standards' (2009) 36 (4) European Review of Agricultural Economics, pp. 525–539.

MCGEE, ANDREW/WEATHERHILL, STEPHEN, 'The Evolution of the Single Market: Harmonisation or Liberalisation?' (1990) 53 The Modern Law Review, pp. 578–596.

METCALFE, LES, 'Reforming the European Governance: Old Problems or New Principles?' (2001) 67 International Review of Administrative Sciences, pp. 415–443.

MITCHELL, ANDREW, Legal Principles in WTO Disputes, Cambridge University Press 2008.

MO, JOHN, 'The Mystery of Market Access' in: QURESHI ASIF/GAO XUAN, International Economic Law – Critical Concepts in Law, Vol. III, World Trade Law, Routledge, pp. 50–76.

MÖLLERS, CHRISTOPH, 'European Governance: Meaning and Value of a Concept' (2006) 43 Common Market Law Review, pp. 313–336.

NORER, ROLAND, 'Europäisierung des schweizerischen Agrarrechts: zwischen bilateralen Abkommen und autonomen Nachvollzug' in: CARONI, MARTINA/HESELHAUS, SEBASTIAN/MATHIS, KLAUS /NORER, ROLAND, Auf der Schölle und in lichten Höhen: Festschrift für Paul Richli zum 65. Geburtstag, Dike Verlag 2011, pp. 569–590.

O'ROURKE, RAYMOND, European Food Law, 3rd ed., Sweet and Maxwell 2005.

ORGANISATION FOR ECONOMIC COOPERATION AND DEVELOPMENT (OECD), Corporate Governance: Improving Competitiveness and Access to Capital in Global Markets, OECD, Paris 1998.

ORGANISATION FOR ECONOMIC COOPERATION AND DEVELOPMENT (OECD), Final Report on Private Standards and the Shaping of Agro-Food Systems, Paris, Working Party on Agricultural Policies and Markets, 2006.

ORGANISATION FOR ECONOMIC COOPERATION AND DEVELOPMENT (OECD), Participatory Development and Good Governance, Paris OECD 1994.

PAUWELYN, JOOST, 'Rule-Based Trade 2.0? The Rise of Informal Rules and International Standards and How They May Outcompete WTO Treaties' (2014) 14 Journal of International Economic Law, pp. 1–13.

PELKMANS, JACQUES, 'The New Approach to Technical Harmonization and Standardization' (1987) 25 Journal of Common Market Studies, pp. 249–269.

PERI, CLAUDIO, 'The Universe of Food Quality' (2006) 1–2 Food Quality and Preferences, pp. 3–8.

PERLMAN, MARK, The Pillars of Economic Understanding: Ideas and Traditions, The University of Michigan Press 1998.

PEUKERT, ALEXANDER, 'The Competitive Significance of Collective Trademarks' in: ROSEN, JAN (ed), Individualism and Collectiveness in Intellectual Property Law, Edward Elgar Publishing 2012, pp. 241–254.

PIRES DE CARVAHLO, NUNO, The TRIPS Regime of Trademarks and Designs, 2nd ed., Kluwer Law International 2006.

POWER, MICHAEL, The Audit Society: Rituals of Verification, Oxford University Press 1997.

PRÈVOST, DENISE, 'Private Sector Food Safety Standards and the SPS Agreement: Challenges and Possibilities' (2008) 33 South African Yearbook of International Law, pp. 1–37.

PRÉVOST, DENISE/VAN DEN BOSSCHE, PETER, 'The Agreement on the Application of Sanitary and Phytosanitary Measures' in: MACRORY, PATRICK/APPLETON, ARTHUR/ PLUMMER, MICHAEL (eds), The World Trade Organization: Legal, Economic and Political Analysis, Springer 2005, pp. 231–370.

QUICK, REINHARD/BLUNTHER, ANDREAS, 'Has the Appellate Body erred? An Appraisal and Criticism of the Ruling in the WTO Hormones Case' (1999) Journal of International Economic Law, pp. 603–639.

RAMSEY, LISA, 'Descriptive Trademarks and the First Amendment' (2005) 10 Tennessee Law Review, pp. 1110–1121.

RICARDO, DAVID, The Principles of Political Economy and Taxation, 1819, reprinted by Dent & Sons Ltd./Charles E. Tuttle Co. 1973.

ROSENAU, JAMES, 'Governance, Order, and Change in World Politics' in: ROSENAU, JAMES/CZEMPOIEL, ERNST-OTTO (eds), Governance without Government: Order and Change in World Politics, Cambridge University Press 1992, pp. 1–29.

SABEL, CHARLES/ZEITLIN, JONATHAN, 'Learning from Difference: The New Architecture of Experimentalist Governance in the EU' (2008) 14 European Law Journal, pp. 271–327.

SANDER, GERALD, 'Codex Alimentarius Commission (CAC)', in: WOLFRUM RÜDIGER (ed), The Max Planck Encyclopedia of Public International Law, Vol. II, Oxford University Press 2012.

SCHARPF, FRITZ, 'European Governance: Common Concerns vs. the Challenge of Diversity' in: JOERGES, CHRISTIAN/MENY, YYES/WEILER, JOSEPH (eds), Mountain or Molehill: Critical Appraisal of the Commission White Paper on Governance, Jean Monnet Working Paper 6/01, New York University 2001, pp. 1–12.

SCHECHTER, FRANK I., 'The Rational Basis of Trademark Protection' (1926) 40 Harvard Law Review, pp. 813–833.

SCHMIDT, SUSAN, 'Mutual Recognition as a New Mode of Governance' (2007) 14 (5) Journal of European Public Policy, pp. 367–381.

SCHMIDT-PFINTZER, JAN, 'Article 15' in: STOLL, PETER-TOBIAS/BUSCHE, JAN/AREND, KATRIN (eds), WTO – Trade Related Aspects of Intellectual Property Rights, Max Planck Commentaries on World Trade Law, Martinus Nijhoff Publishers 2009, pp. 306–315.

SCOTT, JOANNE, Commentary on the Sanitary and Phytosanitary Measures Agreement, Oxford University Press 2007.

SCOTT, JOANNE, 'International Trade and Environmental Governance: Relating Rules (and Standards) in the EU and the WTO' (2004) 15 (2) European Journal of International Law, pp. 307–354.

SELL, SUSAN, Power and Ideas: North-South Politics of Intellectual Property and Antitrust, State University of New York Press 1998.

SENDEN, LINDA, 'Soft Law, Self-Regulation and Co-Regulation in European Law: Where do They Meet?' (2005) 9 (1) Electronic Journal of Comparative Law, pp. 1–27.

SHAFFER, GREGORY, 'Reconciling Trade and Regulatory Goals: The Prospects and Limits of New Approaches to Transatlantic Governance through the Mutual Recognition and Safe Harbour Agreements' (2002) 9 Columbia Journal of European Law, pp. 29–77.

SHAPIRO, SYDNEY, 'International Trade Agreements, Regulatory Protection and Public Accountability' (2002) 54 (1) Administrative Law Review, pp. 435–457.

SHEPHERSON, SHERRY, Standards, Conformity Assessment and Developing Countries, The World Bank 1997.

SIMAI, MIHALY, The Future of Global Governance: Managing Risks and Change in the International System, US Institute of Peace 1994.

SMITH, ADAM, An Inquiry into the Nature and Causes of the Wealth of Nations, 1776, reprinted by Random House, Inc./Modern Library Ed. 1994.

SMITH, GARY, Interaction of Public and Private Standards in the Food Chain, OECD Food, Agriculture and Fisheries Working Papers Nr. 15, OECD Publishing 2009, AGR/CA/APM(2006)21/final.

STEINBERG, RICHARD, 'Trade-Environment Negotiations in the EU, NAFTA and WTO: Regional Trajectories of Rule Development' (1997) 91 American Journal of International Law 1997, pp. 231–232.

STEPHENSON, SHERRY, Standards and Conformity Assessment as Nontariff Barriers to Trade, Policy Research Working Paper Nr. 1826, The World Bank Development Research Group, September 1997.

STEWART, TERENCE (ed), The GATT Uruguay Round: A Negotiating History, Kluwer Law & Taxation 1993.

STEWART, TERENCE/JOHANSON, DAVID, 'The SPS Agreement of the World Trade Organisation and Interntional Organisations: The Roles of the Codex Alimentarious Commission, the International Plant Protection Convention and the International Office of Epizootics' (1998) 26 Syracuse Journal of International Law, pp. 23–54.

STIM, RICHARD, Patent, Copyright & Trademark: An Intellectual Property Desk Reference, 12th ed., Bang Printing 2012.

STOLL, PETER-TOBIAS/SCHORKOPF, FRANK, WTO: World Economic Order, World Trade Law, Max Plank Institute for Comparative Public and International Law, Martinus Nijhoff Publishers 2003.

STREINZ, RUDOLF, Europarecht, 6th ed., C.F. Müller 2003.

STREINZ, RUDOLF, 'Die Europäisierung des Lebensmittelrechts' in: POLEDNA, THOMAS/ARTER, OLIVIER/GATTIKER, MONIKA, Lebensmittelrecht, Stämpfli 2006, pp. 151–210.

SYKES, ALAN, Product Standards for Internationally Integrated Good Markets, Brookings Institution 1995.

TAMIOTTI, LUDIVINE, 'Article 2 and 3 TBT' in: RÜDIGER, WOLFRUM/STOLL, PETER-TOBIAS/SEIBERT-FOHR, ANJA (eds), WTO – Technical Barriers and SPS Measures, Vol. III, Martinus Hijhoff Publishers 2007, pp. 210–242.

THILMANY, DAWN/BARRETT, CHRISTOPHER, 'Regulatory Barriers in an Integrated World Food Market' (1997) 19 (2) Appl. Econ. Perspect. Pol., pp. 91–107.

TREBILCOCK, MICHAEL/SOLOWAY, JULIE, 'International Trade Policy and Domestic Food Safety Regulation: The Case for Substantial Deference by the WTO Dispute Settlement Body under the SPS Agreement' in: KENNEDY, DANIEL/SOUTHWICK, JAMES (eds), The Political Economy of International Trade Law, Essays in Honor of Robert E. Hudec, Cambridge University Press 2002, pp. 537–574.

TREBILCOCK, MICHAEL/HOWSE, ROBERT/ELIASON, ANTONIA, The Regulation of International Trade, 4th ed., Routledge 2013.

TRÜTEN, DIRK, 'Einfluss des EG-Lebensmittelrechts auf das schweizerische Recht' in: WEBER, ROLF/KLEMM, URS/BAUMGARTNER, TOBIAS/GROLIMUND, NINA/TRÜTEN, DIRK, Lebensmittelrecht EG-Schweiz, Schulthess 2006, pp. 105–126.

UNITED NATIONS DEVELOPMENT PROGRAM (UNDP), 'Governance for Sustainable Development: Integrating Governance in the Post-2015 Development Framework, Discussion Paper' March 2014.

UNITED NATIONS INDUSTRIAL DEVELOPMENT ORGANIZATION (UNIDO), 'Product Quality: A Guide for Small and Medium-Sized Enterprises' Working Paper, Vienna 2006.

VAN DEN BOSSCHE, PETER, The Law and Policy of the World Trade Organization: Text, Cases and Materials, Cambridge University Press 2005.

VAN DER MEULEN, BERND/VAN DER VELDEN, MENNO, European Food Law Handbook, Wageningen Academic Publishers 2008.

VAPNEK, JESSICA/SPREIJ, MELVIN, 'Perspectives and Guidelines on Food Legislation: With a New Model Food Law' FAO Legislative Study 97, FAO 2005.

VEGGELAND, FRODE/BORGEN, SVEN, Changing the Codex: The Role of International Institutions Norwegian Agricultural Economics Research Institute, Oslo, January 2002.

VOGEL, DAVID, Trading Up: Consumer and Environmental Regulation in a Global Economy, Harvard University Press 1995.

VON BOGDANDY, ARMIN/DANN, PHILIPP/GOLDMANN, MATTHIAS, 'Developing the Publicness of Public International Law: Towards a Legal Framework for Global Governance Activities' in: VON BOGDANDY, ARMIN/WOLFRUM, RÜDIGER/VON BERNSTORFF, JOCHEN/DANN, PHILIPP/GOLDMANN, MATTHIAS (eds), The Exercise of Public Authority by International Institutions, Springer 2006, pp. 3–32.

VOON, TANIA/MITCHELL, ANDREW/GASCOIGNE, CATHERINE, 'Consumer Information, Consumer Preferences and Product Labels under the TBT Agreement' in: TREBILCOCK, MICHAEL/EPPS, TRACEY (eds), Research Handbook on the WTO and Technical Barriers to Trade, Edward Elgar 2013, pp. 454–484.

VOS, ELLEN, 'EU Food Safety Regulation in the Aftermath of the BSE Crisis' (2000) 23 Journal of Consumer Policy, pp. 227–255.

WALLIS, RICHARD, Guide to European Law and Institutions, Straightforward Publishing 2007.

WEISS, THOMAS, 'Governance, Good Governance and Global Governance: Conceptual and Actual Changes' in: QURESHI, ASIF/GAO, XUAN (eds), International Economic Law: Critical Concepts in Law, Vol. V, International Development Law, Routledge 2001, pp. 390–413.

WIJKSTROM, ERIK/MCDANIELS, DEVIN, 'International Standards and the WTO TBT Agreement: Improving Governance for Regulatory Alignment' World Trade Organization, Economic Research and Statistics Division, Staff Working Paper ERSD, 25 April 2013.

WILKOF, NEIL/BURKITT, DANIEL, Trade Mark Licensing, 2nd ed., Sweet & Maxwell 2005.

WILLIAMSON, OLIVER, 'The Economics of Governance: Framework and Implications' (1984) 140 Zeitschrift für die gesamte Staatswissenschaft, pp. 195–223.

WORLD INTELLECTUAL PROPERTY ORGANISATION (WIPO), WIPO Intellectual Property Handbook: Policy, Law and Use, 2nd ed., 2004.

WIRTH, DAVID, 'The Role of Science in the Uruguay Round and NAFTA Trade Disciplines' (1994) 27 Cornell International Law Journal, pp. 817–859.

WORLD BANK, Governance – The World Bank's Experience, Washington DC: The World Bank 1994.

WORLD HEALTH ORGANIZATION (WHO), Global Strategy for Food Safety, Food Safety Programs, Geneva, WHO 2002.

WORLD TRADE ORGANIZATION, Understanding the WTO, Geneva 2011.

YOUNG, ALASDAIR, 'The Politics of Regulation and the Internal Market' in: JORGENSEN, KNUD/POLLACK, MARK/ROSAMOND, BEN (eds), Handbook of European Union Politics, Sage Publications Ltd. 2007, pp. 373–394.

YOUNG, ORAN, International Governance: Protecting the Environment in a Stateless Society, Cornell University Press 1994.

ZÄCH, ROGER, 'Gesamtüberblick' in: THÜRER, DANIEL/WEBER, ROLF/ZÄCH, ROGER, Bilaterale Verträge EG-Schweiz: Ein Handbuch, Schultess 2002, pp. 3–15.

ZUMBANSEN, PEER, 'The Incurable Constitutional Itch: Transnational Private Regulatory Governance and the Woes of Legitimacy', King's Collge London Dickson Poon School of Law Legal Studies Research Paper Series, Nr. 2014–40.

Legal Materials

GATT Case Law

GATT, *Belgium Family Allowances*, Decision of 6 November 1952, G/32 – 1S/59.

GATT, *Italian Discrimination Against Agricultural Machinery (Italy – Agricultural Machinery)*, 15 July 1958, L/833 – 7S/60.

GATT, *Generalized System of Preferences*, Decision of 25 June 1971, BISD 18S/24.

GATT, *European Economic Community (EEC) Measures on Animal Feed Proteins*, Decision of 2 December 1977, L/4599 – 25S/49.

GATT, *Differential and More Favourable Treatment, Reciprocity and Fuller Participation of Developing Countries*, Decision of 28 November 1979, L/4903.

GATT, *United States – Section 337 of the Tariff Act of 1930 (US – Section 337)*, Decision of 16 January 1980, L/6439 – 36S/345.

GATT, *Spain Tariff Treatment on Unroasted Coffee*, Decision of 27 April 1981, L/5135 – 28S/102.

GATT, *Unites States Customer User Fee*, Decision of 25 November 1987, L/6264 – 35S/245.

GATT, *Japan – Trade in Semi-Conductors*, Decision of 4 May 1988, L/6309 – 35S/116.

GATT, *European Economic Community (EEC) – Restrictions on Imports of Dessert Apples* (Complaint by Chile), Decision of 18 April 1989, L/6491 – 36S/93.

GATT, *United States Section 337 of the Tariff Act of 1939*, Decision of 7 November 1989, L/6439, BISD36S/345.

GATT, *United States Denial of Most-Favoured-Nation Treatment as to Non-Rubber Footwear from Brazil*, Decision of 10 January 1992, DS18/R – 39S/128.

GATT, *Tokyo Round Committee on TBT, Termination of the Tokyo Round Agreement on Technical Barriers to Trade*, Decision of 20 October 1995, TBT/40 Special Distribution.

WTO Case Law

Panel Reports

WTO Panel Report, *European Communities – Measures Concerning Meat and Meat Products (United States)*, 18 August 1997, WT/DS26/R/USA.

WTO Panel Report, *European Communities – Measures Concerning Meat and Meat Products (Canada)*, 18 August 1997, WT/DS48/R/CAN.

WTO Panel Report, *Japan – Measures Affecting Consumer Photographic Film and Paper*, 22 April 1998, WT/DS44/R.

WTO Panel Report, *Indonesia – Certain Measures Affecting the Automobile Industry*, 2 July 1998, WT/DS54/55/59/64/R.

WTO Panel Report, *Canada – Patent Protection of Pharmaceutical Products*, 17 March 2000, WT/DS114/R.

WTO Panel Report, *United States – Section 110(5) of the US Copyright Act*, 15 June 2000, WT/DS160/R.

WTO Panel Report, *Argentina – Measures Affecting the Export of Bovine Hides and the Import of Finished Leather (Argentina – Hides and Leather)*, 19 December 2000, WT/DS155/R.

WTO Panel Report, *European Communities (EC) – Trade Definition of Sardines*, 29 May 2002, WT/DS231/R.

WTO Panel Report, *European Communities (EC) – Protection of Trademarks and Geographical Indications for Agricultural Products and Foodstuffs (Australia)*, 15 March 2005, WT/DS290/R.

WTO Panel Report, *European Communities (EC) – Protection of Trademarks and Geographical Indications for Agricultural Products and Foodstuffs (United States)*, 15 March 2005, WT/DS174/R.

WTO Panel Report, *United States – Measures concerning the Importation, Marketing and Sale of Tuna and Tuna Products*, 15 September 2011, WT/DS381/R.

Appellate Body Reports

WTO Appellate Body Report, *United States – Standards for Reformulated and Conventional Gasoline*, 29 April 1996, WT/DS2/AB/R.

WTO Appellate Body Report, *Japan – Taxes on Alcoholic Beverages*, 4 October 1996, WT/DS8/AB/R, WT/DS10/11AB/R.

WTO Appellate Body Report, *Canada – Certain Measures Concerning Periodicals*, 30 June 1997, WT/DS31/AB/R.

WTO Appellate Body, *European Communities (EC) – Regime for the Importation, Sale and Distribution of Bananas*, 9 September 1997, WT/DS27/AB/R.

WTO Appellate Body, *European Communities (EC) – Measures Concerning Meat and Meat Products*, 16 January 1998, WT/DS26/AB/R.
WTO Appellate Body Report, *United States – Import Prohibition of Certain Shrimp and Shrimp Products*, 12 October 1998, WT/DS58/AB/R.
WTO Appellate Body, *Australia-Measures Affecting the Importation of Salmon*, 20 October 1998, WT/DS18/AB/R.
WTO Appellate Body Report, *Korea – Taxes on Alcoholic Beverages*, 18 January 1999, WT/DS84/AB/R.
WTO Appellate Body Report, *Japan – Measures Affecting Agricultural Products*, 19 March 1999, WT/DS76/AB/R.
WTO Appellate Body Report, *United States – Section 211 Omnibus Appropriations Act of 1998*, 2 January 2001, WT/DS176/AB/R.
WTO Appellate Body Report, *Korea – Measures Affecting the Importation of Fresh, Chilled and Frozen Beef*, 10 January 2001, WT/DS161/AB/R.
WTO Appellate Body Report, *European Communities (EC) – Measures Affecting Asbestos and Asbestos-Containing Products*, 12 March 2001, WT/DS135/AB/R.
WTO Appellate Body, *United States – Section 211 Omnibus Appropriations Act of 1998*, 2 January 2002, WT/DS176/AB/R.
WTO Appellate Body, *European Communities (EC) – Trade Definition of Sardines*, 26 September 2002, WT/DS231/AB/R.
WTO, Appellate Body Report, *Japan – Measures Affecting the Importation of Apples*, 23 November 2003, WT/DS245/AB/R.
WTO Appellate Body, *European Communities (EC) – Conditions for the Granting of Tariff Preferences to Developing Countries*, 7 April 2004, WT/DS246/AB/R.
WTO Appellate Body, *United States – Measures Affecting the Production and Sale of Clove Cigarettes*, 4 April 2012, WT/DS406/AB/R.
WTO Appellate Body, *United States – Measures Concerning the Importation, Marketing and Sale of Tuna and Tuna Products*, 16 May 2012, WT/DS381/AB/R.
WTO Appellate Body, *United States Certain Country of Origin Labelling (COOL) Requirements*, 29 June 2012, WT/DS384/386/AB/R.

EU Case Law

Procureur du Roi v. Benoit and Gustave Dassonville [1974] Case C-8/74, Judgement of 11 July 1974, ECR 837.
Rewe-Zentral AG v. Bundesmonopolverwaltung für Branntwein [1978] Case C-120/78, Judgement of 20 February 1979, ECR 649.
Frans-Nederlandse Maatschappij Voor Biologische Producten [1981], Case C 272/80, Judgement of 17 December 1981, ECR 3277.

Sandoz [1983], Case C-174/82, Judgment of 14 July 1983, ECR 2445.
European Communities v. Federal Republic of Germany (Reinheitsgebot) [1987], Case C-178/84, Judgment of 12 May 1987, ECR 1227.
Bernhard Keck and Daniel Mithouard [1993] Joined Cases C-267/91 and C-268/91, Judgement of 24 November 1993, ECR I 6097.
Christian Poucet v. Assurances Générales de France and Caisse Mutuelle Régionale du Languedoc-Roussillon [1997] Case C-321/94, Judgement of 7 May 1997, ECR I 2343.
Affish BV v Rijksdienst voor de Keuring van Vee en Vlees [1997], Judgement of 17 July 1997, Case C-183/95, ECR 4315.
Commission of the European Communities v. Federal Republic of Germany [2002] Case C-325/00, Judgement of 5 November 2002, ECR I-9977.
Commission of the European Communities v. Kingdom of Belgium [2006] Case C-433/04, Judgement of 9 November 2006, ECR I 10653.
Massimiliano Placanica and Others [2007] Cases C-338/04, C-359/04 and C-360/04, Judgement of 6 March 2007, ECR I-1891.
Commission of the European Communities v. Federal Republic of Germany [2007] Case C-490/04, Judgement of 18 July 2007, ECR I 6095.
Commission of the European Communities v. Italian Republic [2007] Case C-260/04, Judgement of 13 September 2007, ECR I 708.
Commission of the European Communities v. Italian Republic [2009] Case C-110/05, Judgment of 10 February 2009, ECR I 519.
Jose Manuel Blanco Perez and Maria del Pilar Chao Gomez [2010] Joined Cases C-570/07 and C-571/07, Judgment of 1 June 2010, ECR I 4629.
Commission of the European Communities v. Portugal [2010] Case C-458/08, Judgment of 18 November 2010, ECR I 11599.
Ker Optika bt v. ANTSZ Del-dunanruli Regionalis Intezete [2010] Case C-108/09, Judgment of 25 November 2010, ECR I 1039.

National Case Law

(German) Federal Administrative Court, *ger.* Bundesverwaltungsgericht (BVerwG), Decision of 10 December 1987, 3 C 18.87.
(German) Administrative Court of Aachen, *ger.* Verwaltungsgericht Aachen (VG Aachen), Decision of 30 July 2010, 7 K 1467/09.
(German) Administrative Court of Appeals North-Rhein Westphalia, *ger.* Oberverwaltungsgericht Nordrhein-Westfalen (OVG NWF), Decision of 2 November 2010, 8A 475/10.

(German) Administrative Court of Appeals North-Rhein Westphalia, *ger.* Oberverwaltungsgericht Nordrhein-Westfalen (OVG NWF), Decision of 16 November 2010, 13A 2108/10.

Primary Legislation

Multilateral Treaties

Paris Convention for the Protection of Industrial Property, 20 March 1883, UNTS 305.

Berne Convention for the Protection of Literary and Artistic Works, 9 September 1886.

Agreement on Technical Barriers to Trade, 12 April 1979, 1186 UNTS 276, GATT, BISD, 26th Supp 8 (1980).

WIPO Treaty on Intellectual Property in Respect of Integrated Circuits, 26 May 1989.

Mercado Común del Sur (MERCOSUR), *en.* Southern Common Market, 26 March 1991.

North American Free Trade Agreement (NAFTA), 17 December 1992.

Association of Southeast Asian Nations (ASEAN), 28 January 1992.

General Agreement on Tariffs and Trade 1994 (GATT), 15 April 1994, Marrakesh Agreement Establishing the World Trade Organization, Annex 1A, 1867 UNTS 187.

Agreement on Trade-Related Aspects of Intellectual Property Rights, 1 January 1995, 1869 UNTS 299.

Marrakesh Agreement Establishing the World Trade Organization, 1 January 1995, 1867 UNTS 154.

Agreement on Technical Barriers to Trade, 1 January 1995, 1868 UNTS 120.

Agreement on Sanitary and Phytosanitary Measures, 1 January 1995, 1867 UNTS 493.

WHO Framework Convention on Tobacco Control, 21 May 2003, UNTS 2302, 166.

European Parliament, Treaty on the Functioning of the European Union, 9 May 2008, OJ C 115/47.

Bilateral Treaties

Agreement on the Creation of the European Free Trade Association, 4 January 1960, SR 0.632.31.

Agreement between the Swiss Confederation and the European Economic Communities, 22 July 1972, SR 0.632.401.

Agreement between the European Communities and its Member States of the one part, and of the Swiss Confederation of the other, on the Free Movement of Persons 21 June 1999, SR 0.142.112.681.

Agreement between the European Communities and the Swiss Confederation on Certain Aspects of Government Procurement, 21 June 1999, SR 0.172.052.68.

Agreement between the European Communities and the Swiss Confederation on the Carriage of Goods and Passengers by Rail and Road, 21 June 1999, SR 0.740.72.

Agreement between the European Communities and the Swiss Confederation on Trade in Agricultural Products, 21 June 1999, SR 0.916.026.81.

Agreement between the European Communities and the Swiss Confederation on Air Transport, 20 April 2002, OJ L 114.

Agreement between the European Communities and the Swiss Confederation on Mutual Recognition in relation to Conformity Assessment, 30 April 2002, OJ L 114.

Agreement between the EC and the Swiss Confederation amending the Agreement between the European Economic Community and the Swiss Confederation of 22 July 1972 as regards the provisions applicable to processed agricultural products, 26 January 2005, OJ L 023.

Agreement between the EC and the Swiss Confederation amending the Agreement between the European Economic Community and the Swiss Confederation of 22 July 1972 as regards the provision applicable to agricultural products, 26 January 2005, SR 0.632.401.23, OJ L 023.

Agreement on Scientific and Technological Cooperation between the European Communities and the European Atomic Energy Community of the one part, and the Swiss Confederation of the other part, 25 June 2007, SR 0.420.513.1.

Agreement between the European Communities and the Swiss Confederation concerning the criteria and mechanisms for establishing the State responsible for examining a request for asylum lodged in a Member State or in Switzerland (Dublin), 27 February 2008, OJ L 53.

Agreement between the European Union, the European Communities and the Swiss Confederation on the Swiss Confederation's Association with the Implementation, Application and Development of the Schengen Acquis (Schengen), 27 February 2008, OJ L 53.

EU Legislation

European Parliament, Reg. (EC) Nr. 178/2002 of 28 January 2002 on the General Principles and Requirements of Food Law, establishing the European Food Safety Authority and laying down Procedures in matters of Food Safety, OJ L 31/1.

EUROPEAN PARLIAMENT Reg. (EC) Nr. 1829/2003 of 22 September 2003 on Genetically Modified Food and Feed, OJ L 268/1.

EUROPEAN PARLIAMENT, COUNCIL AND COMMISSION, Inter-Institutional Agreement on Better Law-Making [2003] OJ C 321/01, 31 December 2003.

EUROPEAN PARLIAMENT, Reg. (EC) Nr. 852/2004 of 29 April 2004 on the Hygiene of Foodstuffs, OJ L 139/1.

EUROPEAN PARLIAMENT, Reg. (EC) Nr. 853/2004 of 29 April 2004 on Hygiene for Food of Animal Origin, OJ L 226/22.

EUROPEAN PARLIAMENT, Reg. (EC) Nr. 854/2004 of 29 April 2004 on Official Controls on Products of Animal Origin intenten for Human Consumption, OJ L 226/83.

EUROPEAN PARLIAMENT, Reg. (EC) Nr. 396/2005 of 23 February 2005 on Maximum Residue Levels of Pesticides in or on Food and Feed of Plant and Animal Origin, OJ L 70/1.

EUROPEAN PARLIAMENT, Reg. (EC) Nr. 764/2008 of 9 July 2008 on the Procedures relating to the Application of Certain National Technical Rules to Products lawfully marketed in another Member State, OJ L 218/21.

EUROPEAN PARLIAMENT, Reg. (EC) Nr. 1333/2008 of 16 December 2008 on Food Additives, OJ L 354/16.

EUROPEAN PARLIAMENT, EU Reg. Nr. 1169/2011 of 25 October 2011 on the Provision of Food Information to Consumers, OJ L 304/18.

National Legislation

(German) Food Law, 1 September 2005, *ger.* Lebensmittel- und Futtermittel-Gesetzbuch, BGBl. I S. 1426.

(German) Freedom of Information Act, *ger.* Gesetz zur Regelung des Zugangs zu Informationen des Bundes (Informationsfreiheitsgesetz – IFG), 5 September 2005, BGBl. I S. 2722.

(Swiss) Federal Act on Technical Barriers to Trade, *ger*. Bundesgesetz vom 6. Oktober 1995 über die technischen Handelshemmnissen, SR 946.51.

(Swiss) Federal Decree on the placement on the market of products manufactured according to foreign technical standards and their control in in the market, *ger*. Veordnung über das Inverkehrbringen von nach ausländischen technischen Vorschriften hergestellten Produkten und über deren Überwachung auf dem Markt (VIPaV), 19 May 2010, SR 946.513.8.

GATT Documents

GATT, Ministerial Declaration on the Uruguay Round (Punta del Este Declaration), 20 September 1986, BISD 33S/19 (1987).

GATT, Standards and Principles concerning the Availability, Scope and Use of Trade-Related Aspects of Intellectual Property Rights, 10 July 1989, MTN.GNG/NG11/W/37.

GATT, Submission by Brazil, 31 October 1988, MTG.GNG/NG11/W/30.

GATT, European Communities (EC) – Draft TRIPS Agreement, 29 March 1990, MTN.GNG/NG11/W/68.

GATT, United States – Draft TRIPS Agreement, 11 May 1990, MTN.GNG/NG11/W70.

WTO Documents

Committee on Sanitary and Phytosanitary Measures, Summary of the Meeting Held on 29–30 June 2005, Note by the Secretariat, 18 August 2005, G/SPS/R37/Rev. 1.

Committee on Sanitary and Phytosanitary Measures, Private Standards and the SPS Agreement, Note of the Secretariat, 24 January 2007, G/SPS/W/246.

Committee on Sanitary and Phytosanitary Measures, Private Industry Standards, Communication from Saint Vincent and the Grenadines, 28 February 2007, G/SPS/GEN/766.

Committee on Sanitary and Phytosanitary Measures, Private and Commercial Standards, Statement by Ecuador at the Meeting of 27–28 June 2007, 5 July 2007, G/SPS/GEN/792.

Committee on Sanitary and Phytosanitary Measures, Private Voluntary Standards Within the WTO Multilateral Framework, Submission by the United Kingdom to the Committee on Sanitary and Phytosanitary Measures, 9 October 2007, WTO/G/SPS/GEN/802.

Committee on Sanitary and Phytosanitary Measures, Questionnaire on SPS-Related Private Standards, Note of the Secretariat, 8 December 2008, G/SPS/W/232.

Committee on Sanitary and Phytosanitary Measures, Effects of SPS-Related Private Standards: Descriptive Report, Note of the Secretariat, 15 June 2009, G/SPS/GEN/932.

Committee on Sanitary and Phytosanitary Measures, Possible Actions for the SPS Committee Regarding Private SPS Standards, Note of the Secretariat, 20 October 2009, G/SPS/W/247.

Committee on Sanitary and Phytosanitary Measures, Possible Actions for the SPS Committee regarding Private SPS Standards, 5 March 2010, G/SPS/W/247/Rev.1.

Committee on Sanitary and Phytosanitary Measures, Possible Actions for the SPS Committee Regarding SPS-Related Private Standards, Note by the Secretariat, 15 June 2010, G/SPS/W/247/Rev.2.

Committee on Sanitary and Phytosanitary Measures, Possible Actions for the SPS Committee Regarding SPS-Related Private Standards, Note by the Secretariat, 11 October 2010, G/SPS/W/247/Rev.3.

Committee on Sanitary and Phytosanitary Measures, Report of the Ad Hoc Working Group on SPS-Related Private Standards to the SPS Committee, 3 March 2011, G/SPS/W/256.

Committee on Sanitary and Phytosanitary Measures, Actions Regarding SPS-Related Private Standards, Decision of the Committee, 6 April 2011, G/SPS/55.

Committee on Sanitary and Phytosanitary Measures, Monitoring the Use of International Standards, 30 May 2011, G/SPS/GEN/1086.

Committee on Sanitary and Phytosanitary Measures SPS Committee, March 2012, G/SPS/W/265 and July 2012, G/SPS/W/265/Rev.1, 28 September 2012, G/SPS/W/265/Rev.2.

Committee on Sanitary and Phytosanitary Measures, Summary of the Meeting 26–27 March 2015, Note by the Secretariat, 21 May 2015, G/SPS/R/78.

WTO, Training Package, Goods: Market Access, WTO 1998.

WTO, Declaration on the TRIPS Agreement and Public Health, Ministerial Conference, 4th Session, Doha, 9–14 November 2001, 20 November 2001, WT/MIN/(01)/DEC/2.

WTO Joint Communication from the European Communities and the United States, EC-Measures concerning Meat and Meat Products (Hormones), 30 September 2009, WT/DS26/28.

WTO, International Trade Statistics 2013, <www.wto.org/statistics> (last visited: 31 March 2014).

FAO/WHO and OECD/FAO Documents

Joint FAO/WHO Conference on Food Standards, Report Session, 1 to 5 October 1962, Geneva, ALINORM 62/8.

Joint FAO/WHO Food Standards Program, Report of the 24th Session, 15 November 2000, Geneva, ALINORM 01/23.

Joint FAO/WHO Conference on Food Standards, Report of the 19th (extraordinary) Session, 17–21 November 2003, Paris, ALINORM 04/27/33.

Joint FAO/WHO Conference on Food Standards, Report of the 22nd Session, 11 to 15 April 2005, Paris, ALINORM 05/28/33A.

Joint FAO/WHO Food Standards Program, Report of the 28th Session 28, 4 to 9 July 2005, Rome, ALINORM 05/28/27.

FAO, Introduction to Codex Alimentarius Commission, Food Quality and Standards Services, Food and Nutrition Division, Module 4, available at: <http://www.fao.org/docrep/003/x7354e/x7354e04.htm>.

OECD/FAO, OECD/FAO Agricultural Outlook 2013–2022, <http://www.agri-outlook.org>.

EU Documents

European Commission

European Commission, General Program for the Elimination of the Technical Barriers to Trade, adopted by the European Council in its Resolution [1969], OJ C-76/1.

European Commission, Communication concerning the Consequences of the Judgment given by the Court of Justice on 20 February 1979 in Case 120/78 (Cassis de Dijon), OJ C 256/2, 3 October 1980.

European Commission, White Paper on Completing the Single Market, 14 June 1985, COM(85)310 final.

European Commission, Community Legislation on Foodstuffs, 8 November 1985, COM(85)603 final.

European Commission, Green Paper on the Development of Standardisation: Action for Faster Technical Integration in Europe, 8 October 1990, COM(90)456 final.

European Commission, Green Paper on the General Principles of Food Law in the European Union, 30 April 1997, COM(97)176.

European Commission, Communication on Consumer Health and Food Safety, 30 April 1997, COM(97)183 final.

European Commission, Communication on the Mutual Recognition in the Context of the Follow-up to the Action Plan for the Single Market, 16 June 1999, COM(1999)299 final.

European Commission, White Paper on Food Safety, 12 January 2000, COM(99)719.

European Commission, Enhancing the Implementation of New Approach Directives, 7 May 2003, COM(2003)240.

European Commission, Guidance Document on the Application of the Mutual Recognition Regulation (EC) 764/2008 to Food Supplements, 1 February 2010, available at: <http://ec.europa.eu/enterprise/policies/single-market-goods/files/mutual-recognition/food-supplements/food-supplements_en.pdf>.

European Commission, European Governance: A White Paper, 12 October 2011, COM(201) 428 final, OJ C 287/1.

European Council

EUROPEAN COUNCIL, Resolution on Industrial Policy, 17 December 1973, OJ C 117.

EUROPEAN COUNCIL, Council Directive 92/59/EEC on General Product Safety, 19 June 1992, OJ L 228/24.

EUROPEAN COUNCIL, 2094th Council Meeting on the Internal Market, Press Release, 18 May 1998, available at: <http://europa.eu/rapid/press-release_PRES-98-148_en.htm>.

EUROPEAN COUNCIL, Resolution of 28 October 1999 on Mutual Recognition, 19 May 2000, OJ C 141.

Other Materials

German Food Code Commission, Rules of Procedure, 25 May 2009, *ger.* Geschäftsordnung der Deutschen Lebensmittelbuch-Kommission; available at: <https://www.bmel.de/SharedDocs/Downloads/Ernaehrung/Lebensmittelbuch/GeschaeftsordnungLebensmittelbuchkommission.pdf;jsessionid=2BD74FB6EEF B370C315A 83D89D9F2879.2_cid358?__blob=publicationFile>.

ISO 22000, Food Safety Management Systems: Requirements for Any Organization on the Food Chain; available at: <http://www.iso.org/iso/home/store/catalogue_tc/catalogue_detail.htm?csnumber=35466>.

ISO Membership Manual, August 2013, available at: <http://www.iso.org/iso/iso_membership_manual_2013.pdf>.

ISO Standard-Setting Process; available at: <http://www.iso.org/iso/home/standards_development/resources-for-technical-work/stages_of_the_development_of_international_standards.htm>.

ISO Statutes, 17th Ed., 2013; available at: <http://www.iso.org/iso/statutes.pdfg>.

ISO Technical Specification ISO 22005: 2007, Traceability in the Feed and Food Chain: General Principles and Basic Requirements for System Design and Implementation; available at: <http://www.iso.org/iso/home/store/catalogue_tc/catalogue_detail.htm?csnumber=36297>.

ISO Technical Specification ISO/TS 22002-1/4:2009, Prerequisites Programs for Food Safety: Catering, Food Manufacturing, Farming and Food Packaging Manufacturing; available at: <http://www.iso.org/iso/home/store/catalogue_tc/catalogue_detail.htm?csnumber=44001>.

ISO Technical Specification ISO/TS 22003:2013, Food Safety Management Systems: Requirements for Bodies providing Audit and Certification of Food Safety Management Systems; available at: <http://www.iso.org/iso/home/store/catalogue_tc/catalogue_detail.htm?csnumber=39835>.

ISO Technical Specification ISO/TS 22004:2005, Food Safety Management Systems: Guidance on the Application of ISO 22000:2005; available at: <http://www.iso.org/iso/home/store/catalogue_tc/catalogue_detail.htm?csnumber=39835>.

ISO, ISO Standards and Food: Quality and Safety from Farm to Fork, January 2012, available at: <http://www.iso.org/iso/iso_and_food.pdf>.

ISO, Standard-Setting Process, available at: <http://www.iso.org/iso/home/standards_development/resources-for-technical-work/stages_of_the_development_of_international_standards.htm>.

ISO, Structure and Governance, available at: <http://www.iso.org/iso/home/about/about_governance.htm>.

ISO, Who Develops ISO Standards, available at: <http://www.iso.org/iso/home/standards_development/who-develops-iso-standards.htm>.

Swiss Confederation, Federal Department of Foreign Affairs (FDFA), Bilateral Agreements Switzerland-EU, 17 August 2009, available at: <http://www.europa.admin.ch/index.html?lang=en>.

Swiss Confederation, Federal Department of Foreign Affairs (FDFA), Bilateral Agreements Switzerland-EU: Fact Sheets, 2 November 2007, available at: <www.bundespublikationen.admin.ch>.

Webster's New World Dictionary, William Collins & World Publishing Co., Inc. 1976.

Studies in Global Economic Law
Studien zum globalen Wirtschaftsrecht
Études en droit économique mondial

Present and future economic, technological and societal changes and evolutions fundamentally affect traditional legal structures of the territorial state system. They increasingly call for global approaches and solutions, transgressing the tools of classical public international law. This trilingual series publishes monographs, studies and collected papers dedicated to these challenges. The contributions examine existing instruments, in particular within the framework of the international trading system. They explore new approaches and search for innovative solutions within the global process of legal integration. Research efforts are dedicated to different walks of life and areas of regulation, and to the quest for adequate constitutional structures of transnational and democratic processes.

Wirtschaftliche, technologische und gesellschaftliche Entwicklungen der Gegenwart und Zukunft bewirken tiefgreifende Änderungen traditioneller Strukturen des Rechts des Territorialstaats und rufen zunehmend nach globalen Vorgehensweisen und Lösungen, die oftmals über das Instrumentarium des klassischen Völkerrechts hinaus weisen. Die dreisprachige Reihe publiziert Monographien, Studien und Tagungsbände, die sich vertieft mit diesen Herausforderungen auseinandersetzen. Die Beiträge untersuchen das bestehende Instrumentarium namentlich im Rahmen des Welthandelssystems und forschen nach neuen Ansätzen und Lösungen im Rahmen des globalen Integrationsprozesses. Dazu gehören Studien zu den Regelungen einzelner Sach- und Lebensbereiche wie auch zu Fragen adäquater transnationaler demokratischer Verfassungs- und Entscheidungsstrukturen.

Les évolutions actuelles et futures sur le plan technique, économique et social ne cesseront d'influencer profondément les structures traditionnelles du droit de l'état territorial. Par conséquent, des approches et des solutions dépassant les instruments du droit international public classique deviennent de plus en plus nécessaires. Cette collection trilingue publie des monographies, études et actes de colloques qui analysent et font face à ces défis. Les contributions examinent les instruments existants, notamment dans la domaine du système commercial mondiale. Elles cherchent à développer des approches nouvelles et des solutions innovatrices dans le contexte du processus d'intégration globale en incluant des études de droit touchant aux différents secteurs et domaines de vie. De plus, les travaux de recherche seront également destinés à trouver les procédures consti-tutionnelles et décisionnelles les plus adéquates et démocratiques au niveau transnational.

Studies in Global Economic Law
Studien zum globalen Wirtschaftsrecht
Études en droit économique mondial

edited by Thomas Cottier

Vol. 1 Martin A. Girsberger – Biodiversity and the Concept of Farmers' Rights in International Law. Factual Background and Legal Analysis, 1999

Vol. 2 David Wyss – Bankdienstleistungen im Allgemeinen Dienstleistungsabkommen der WTO. Auswirkungen auf das schweizerische Bankenrecht, 1999

Vol. 3 Benoît Merkt – Harmonisation internationale et entraide administrative internationale en droit de la concurrence. Droit du GATT/OMC, droit européen, accords bilatéraux et perspectives pour le droit suisse, 2000

Vol. 4 Ingo Meitinger – Der Schutz von Geschäftsgeheimnissen im globalen und regionalen Wirtschaftsrecht. Stand und mögliche Entwicklungen der internationalen und regionalen Rechtsharmonisierung, 2001

Vol. 5 Joëlle de Sépibus – Die Umweltschutzsubvention im Gemeinschaftsrecht. Eine umweltrechtliche Kritik der europäischen Beihilfekontrolle, 2003

Vol. 6 Bobjoseph Mathew – The WTO Agreements on Telecommunications, 2003

Vol. 7 Lukas Engelberger – Die unmittelbare Anwendbarkeit des WTO-Rechts in der Schweiz. Grundlagen und Perspektiven im Kontext internationaler Rechtsentwicklungen, 2004

Vol. 8 Thomas M. Fischer – Die Entbündelung der letzten Meile in der Schweiz im Lichte des GATS, 2004

Vol. 9 Dae-Won Kim – Non-Violation Complaints in WTO Law. Theory and Practice, 2006

Vol. 10 Qi Zhang – Consultation within WTO Dispute Settlement. A Chinese Perspective, 2007

- Vol. 11 FELIX BLOCH – Technologietransfer zum internationalen Umweltschutz. Eine völkerrechtliche Untersuchung unter besonderer Berücksichtigung des Schutzes der Ozonschicht und des Weltklimas, 2007
- Vol. 12 BETTINA BECK – Die Regelung von Slots (Zeitnischen) im Luftverkehrsrecht. Vergabe, Übertragung und Anfechtung in der Schweiz und der EG unter rechtsvergleichender Berücksichtigung US-amerikanischer Normen, 2008
- Vol. 13 SABINA NÜESCH – Voluntary Export Restraints in WTO and EU Law. Consumers, Trade Regulation and Competition Policy, 2010
- Vol. 14 CHUYANG LIU – Maritime Transport Services in the Law of the Sea and the World Trade Organization, 2009
- Vol. 15 MARIELLA MAIDANA-ELETTI – Global Food Governance. Implications of Food Safety and Quality Standards in International Trade Law, 2016